MW01633041

A master of "show, don't tell," Pastor Eric Peterson invites his congregation to attend to God through the liturgies of daily life. Transparent about his own struggles while inviting people into deeper faith, Pastor Eric is a fellow pilgrim on the journey, pointing us all toward the God who holds us. Warm, invitational, and rich, this is a book to be savored.

MARY S. HULST, chaplain at Calvin College

"Grace and peace" is Eric's consistent complementary close for each letter contained in this pastoral epistle, and it's also a great summary of his writing herein. Eric believes that the congregation is the anchor point from which we live out the dynamics of a baptized life, sending us out as salt and light into all the world. Kudos to Eric, and congratulations for receiving the story and metaphor baton so faithfully from his beloved father and mentor.

STEPHEN A. MACCHIA, founder and president of Leadership Transformations; author of fifteen books, including *Becoming a Healthy Church*, *Crafting a Rule of Life*, and *Broken and Whole*

In a series of letters to his congregation, Eric Peterson explores—with great insight—the issues we all face as humans and as believers who live together in community. His memorable turns of phrase and apt metaphors are just what we need in our current culture of divisiveness to remember and embrace the transcendent unity to which Christ calls us.

KELLYE FABIAN, author of *Sacred Questions: A Transformative Journey through the Bible*

In these remarkable letters, I heard both Psalms and Epistles, both Oswald Chambers and Thomas Merton, both anguish and praise, both sacramental hope and nagging doubt. With humility and humanity and honesty, Eric invites his congregants to remember their baptisms, to know that the Lord is good, to do what Christ followers must do. He is a finder, and he invites his congregation—and us—to find. He finds doxology in earth and sky, in joy and anguish, in all the places we seldom see cause for praise. I read these letters along with my morning prayers. Their poetic tones followed the Lectionary Collects seamlessly. At first, I read four letters each morning. As I neared the book's end, I found myself slowing and savoring, almost dreading the word *Epilogue*. I will read them again . . . and again. Without question, the hearts and minds of every pastor and every congregation who gets in on the savoring will benefit immensely from the warm light of these beautiful letters.

BILL ROBINSON, president emeritus of Whitworth University

In a world mass-producing books spacious in rhetorical rhinestones but spare and scarce in true gemstones, Eric Peterson has gifted us with a rarity: a diadem book of gems, each stone highly refractive of Christ. There are ruby-red chapters, brilliantly colored and translucent with truth; sapphire-blue chapters, lustrous and gleaming with beauty; ancient-demantoid missives, dazzling color bursts of love with hidden horsetail occlusions that only reveal themselves when you read slowly and open yourself to the mysteries of woundedness. You cannot help but experience new dimensions of the divine when you adorn your life with this diadem book.

LEONARD SWEET, author of *Rings of Fire*; professor (Drew, George Fox, Tabor, Evangelical); founder/chief contributor to preachthestory.com

LETTERS
— to a —
YOUNG CONGREGATION

Nurturing the growth of a faithful church

ERIC E. PETERSON

A NavPress resource published in alliance with Tyndale House Publishers

NavPress is the publishing ministry of The Navigators, an international Christian organization and leader in personal spiritual development. NavPress is committed to helping people grow spiritually and enjoy lives of meaning and hope through personal and group resources that are biblically rooted, culturally relevant, and highly practical.

For more information, visit NavPress.com.

Letters to a Young Congregation: Nurturing the Growth of a Faithful Church

A NavPress resource published in alliance with Tyndale House Publishers

The Team:
Don Pape, Publisher; David Zimmerman, Acquisitions Editor; Elizabeth Schroll, Copy Editor; Ron C. Kaufmann, Designer

For information about special discounts for bulk purchases, please contact Tyndale House Publishers at csresponse@tyndale.com, or call 1-800-323-9400.

ISBN 978-1-64158-115-8

Printed in the United States of America

26 25 24 23 22 21 20
7 6 5 4 3 2 1

For

Eugene Hoiland Peterson

1932–2018

CONTENTS

INTRODUCTION

As an eagle stirs up its nest, and hovers over its young . . .

DEUTERONOMY 32:11

THEY DON'T KNOW IT at the time, but eagles are born to fly. When the time is right—after ten to twelve weeks, on average—mother eagles begin to dismantle the nest around the eaglets. Sometimes the mother will even nudge the eaglets out of the nest, although the nest gradually becomes uncomfortable enough that the eaglets will leave on their own. That's when they begin to fly. It's an instinct they have that kicks in the moment they start free-falling.

Churches—in stark contrast—do not have such instincts. By appearances, they don't even have much common sense when it comes to the tasks of incarnating the body of Christ in the world through acts of justice, mercy, and love. Consequently, congregations, in their many and diverse forms, need to be instructed in the art of both being and of becoming a beloved community. While human souls were designed to soar, they need to be shown how. We need flight training.

Usually, the way both individuals and congregations

grow into their identity as members of the body of Christ is through trial and error, fits and starts, failure and missteps. Lots of mistakes can be found in the wake of the church's two-thousand-year developmental history. In fact, one of the ways to read and understand that history is through its conflicts and controversies, councils and trials, confessions and declarations, heresies and apologies, detours and errors. When it comes to exhibiting the Kingdom of God, rare are the moments when the church has ever gotten much of it exactly right. It, therefore, is in constant need of guidance. Such guidance is provided both locally and personally.

Although flawed and imperfect themselves, pastors are entrusted with the unique task of attending to the care and cure of souls, as well as giving attention to the health of congregated souls. Lacking ecclesiastical instincts, young churches in particular need instruction and discipline. The art of pastoring involves both encouragement and correction in the way of godliness. Many are the saboteurs that would derail this holy agenda.

I recall an occasion many years ago when I was meeting with my spiritual director. I must have been expressing anxiety about what was going on in our congregation at the time because, uncharacteristically, she interrupted me and said, "Eric, you're being hypervigilant. You need to relax and trust God!" Equally uncharacteristically, I shot back in defense: "You have no idea how inherently fragile congregations are. If somebody's not paying attention to these issues, it could all blow up in a moment. A pastor can't *be* too vigilant!" In my defensiveness, I may have overstated the case, but I still think I was essentially correct: With a variety of forces threatening to do damage, congregations require constant oversight, intervention, correction, and positive reinforcement if they are to grow into healthy expressions of the body of Christ.

The apostle Paul wrote letters to the smattering of congregations he had started around the Mediterranean region in response to issues that were threatening the unity and the purity of the church. It doesn't require sophisticated exegesis to infer that almost all of these letters were prompted by problems. To wit, there was bad theology and bad behavior that crept into these young congregations, threatening to infect the body with a disease which, left untreated, could spread and become deadly. Addressing such issues is prophetic and pastoral work of the highest order. At times the tone we hear is scolding: "You crazy Galatians! Did someone put a spell on you? Have you taken leave of your senses?"[1] Other times the language borders on flattery: "Every time you cross my mind, I break out in exclamations of thanks to God."[2]

Whatever the circumstances, Saint Paul was interested in establishing the first-generation Christians' imaginations and lifestyles in a cosmology as big as the Kingdom of God itself. Following his pastoral lead, I started writing monthly letters to my congregation. It was a new church plant. I was its young pastor. We were going to have to figure out how to grow up together. Nobody told me I had to, nor how to do this, and I didn't have any clear contemporary models to follow. Initially, it was a practical way to connect with our congregation when there was no physical hub to the organization. We rented space on Sunday mornings in a high school. Midweek gatherings were held in people's homes. There were lots of logistics to coordinate and details to communicate during those early formative years.

Over time, especially after we constructed and nested our first-phase building, these congregational communiqués shifted in tone from organizational to inspirational. What you hold in your hand is a selective sampling of essays which span two decades of a young church's growth and development, all of them attempts at developing both a vivid biblical imagination and a faithful lifestyle response.

As I looked back at this collection of letters for the first time recently, I was struck with the realization of how much *I* have learned and grown through the demands and delights placed on me since being pressed into the pastoral vocation. Now well into the third decade of serving the saints and sinners of Colbert Presbyterian Church, I am convinced that this has been the primary environment that has forged me as a child of God. It has been among the supreme gifts of my life to participate in the developmental stages of this young church, for in many ways, we have indeed grown up together. The following collection bears witness to that life and growth in the particularities of people, place, and time.

Toward the end of his life, there were a few occasions when I spoke for my dad. His last public address was a lecture

I delivered for him at Princeton: Jeremiah-like, his words in my mouth. The standing ovation that followed was all for him, though he was thousands of miles away. There were also a handful of times that I wrote for him. As dementia robbed him of his fertile imagination, I did some ghostwriting to help him meet his remaining commitments. The task of a ghostwriter is to communicate the ideas of another, and to do it in their own voice. I'll never forget the first time I did this. After spending half a day attempting to "channel" Eugene, trying to get the words and the voice to sound like him, I pushed back from my desk and said to myself, "I no longer know where his voice ends and mine begins."

I suppose the same could be said for the letters that here follow, and anyone familiar with Eugene's writing will readily detect his influence on mine. My pastoral voice has developed largely through the many years and many conversations we have shared together to the point where it's not always clear just where his ends and mine begins. Although Eugene died on October 22, 2018, I often feel as though he is still overseeing my life and ministry.

In death no less than life, he has been both my father and my bishop. With much gratitude, this volume is dedicated to his memory.

Eric Eugene Peterson
Pentecost, 2020

1

What My Life Is About

MASTER PLAN

These forty years the LORD your God has been with you; you have lacked nothing.

DEUTERONOMY 2:7

THE YEAR 1963 included two related yet not very widely known events. It was the year my parents gave birth to a new church and to a new son: Christ Our King and Eric Eugene. Many people can say that they grew up in the church, but not many people mean it literally. I can. And I do.

During those early, fledgling years, the bedrooms, kitchen, and dining room in our modest-sized house doubled as Sunday-school classrooms. The living room was a frequent gathering place for evening meetings during the week, even a wedding or two! On Sunday mornings my mother would go to the basement, remove the still-damp diapers hanging on a line, toss them in a closet, and set up folding metal chairs for the worship service. Later, when everyone left for their own homes, the diapers would be rehung to finish drying.

I grew up in the church, observing my father as he skillfully executed the pastoral vocation while my mother attended to the liturgies of hospitality and homemaking. There was no separation, no distinction between matters sacred and things secular. After all, if a house could be a church and a laundry room could be a sanctuary, there wouldn't seem to be much, if anything, beyond the reach or the concern of God.

It helped, of course, that my parents' faith was well-integrated, so that who they were on Sunday mornings was no different than at any other time. The man who preached the Word of God in worship was the same one who served up mashed potatoes at our dinner table. The woman who listened to people's problems during the day was the same one who read a book to me and tucked me into bed at night. It was a lifestyle I lived and breathed and enjoyed, even after the church was built just half a mile away. As a result, I came to adopt a worldview that was permeated by awareness of the presence of God in all things and in all people at all times. I suppose that would be considered a blessed upbringing.

As a teenager, when I was ready to get some distance from my younger brother, with whom I shared a room, I moved downstairs. By then it was just a basement again, where we played Ping-Pong and watched television from beanbag chairs, the gatherings for Sunday worship but a memory. My new bedroom was located in what had once been the chancel area. Consequently, there was a white Celtic cross on my closet door. An old, forgotten baptismal font, from which I was claimed as a child of God, sat in a corner. A still older, second-hand organ was there as well. Even the antique Communion table—given by a historic church in Baltimore (presumably when they upgraded to a new one), on which the words "In Remembrance of Me" were carved—was still there, just gathering dust, having been decommissioned as the Lord's Table. Like the ruins of ancient civilizations, these were the remaining vestiges of those holy meetings between God and his people in our basement when I was but a child.

Of course, as a kid, I didn't think it was unusual or strange having those things around. It was just the house I was raised in. And while I was certainly aware that my friends didn't have liturgical furnishings in their bedrooms growing up, I don't think I realized just how much that whole ecclesiastical environment got inside of me until recently. To find myself now as a pastor, therefore, shouldn't (though at times it still does) surprise me. Environmentally, spiritually, socially, even genetically, it would seem that I was predisposed to the pastoral vocation.

The master plan of Christ Our King Presbyterian Church was drawn up by an architect, and over a period of twenty-five years and three building projects, that plan was completed with remarkable accuracy to the original concept. Obviously, it's fairly easy to track the growth and development of a church through the progress of its physical plant. But I am reminded that in my baptism, there is a master plan for Eric Eugene as well, which is continually unfolding and developing. The Chief Architect is none other than my Lord Jesus Christ, who continues to oversee this God-blessed, God-dedicated life and ministry.

So happy fortieth birthday to me. And happy birthday to my old friends in Bel Air, Maryland. May we, over the second forty years of our lives, continue to grow into the master plan of Christ Our King.

Grace and peace,
Pastor Eric

FOR SUCH A PLACE AS THIS

And He will give you the desires of your heart.

PSALM 37:4, NASB

Some folks will tell you they were born at the wrong time in history. Occasionally, for example, I hear people say that they would have been better suited for the simplicity and hard work of a pioneer lifestyle typical of the nineteenth-century westward expansion. Or to live during the Victorian era, particularly with respect to British art and culture.

Me? Being born and raised during the 1960s worked out just fine. The issue wasn't the time, it was the place. I was born in the wrong geography. Without going into the details, I'll just say that there is almost nothing I miss about my native Maryland. Oh, it was fine, as one of the thirteen original colonies go, but my soul was apparently made for something larger.

I fell in love with the Pacific Northwest at an early age. Spending my summers under the Big Sky of Montana, I learned to climb mountains, fish in alpine lakes, and hunt for huckleberries. When I graduated from high school, Whitworth University was my ticket west, followed by a couple of years working as a carpenter in Spokane.

Later, after wrapping up a three-year exile back to the East Coast in order to attend seminary, I found myself in a season of deep discernment: Where would this call on my life take me? Where would the divine Voice send me? I recall one particular moment as I was completing my résumé. On the standardized forms of that day was a page to identify geographical interests. Each of the fifty states and territories of the US were listed individually, along with other countries where the Presbyterian Church had a missionary presence. And then, at the bottom of the page was a lone box next to which were the ominous words "consider me for any opportunity in the world." Because I believed then, as I do now, that my life is not my own, I had no choice but to check that little box with the massive implications. And then, just before I released the manila envelope into the mouth of the mailbox, I prayed, "But Lord, you know my heart is in the Pacific Northwest."

In the intervening weeks, after interviewing with pastoral search committees from Florida to California, I was called first to a well-established church in Tacoma, and then—seven years later—to a not-yet-existent-one in Colbert. Looking back on it now, I don't know that I would have delighted in this blessed vocation nearly as much had I been located in a different place. And in this moment, I simply want to marvel out loud with you over the goodness of our God in answering a whispered prayer on a Princeton street corner twenty-eight years ago, by giving a young man one of the deepest desires of his heart: to be transplanted among the evergreens.

Grace and peace,
Pastor Eric

LISTENING TO LIFE

Silence is not the absence of sound. That would be to imagine it negatively. Silence is a toning down of inner and outer static, noise that occupies not only the ears but also the attention. Silence allows many sounds to reach awareness that otherwise would go unheard—the sounds of birds, water, wind, trees, frogs, insects, and chipmunks, as well as conscience, daydreams, intuitions, inhibitions, and wishes. One cultivates silence not by forcing the ears not to hear, but by turning up the volume on the music of the world and the soul.

THOMAS MOORE, *Meditations: On the Monk Who Dwells in Daily Life*

It was just one year ago that I was welcomed as a guest to the Monastery of Christ in the Desert—the sacred springboard of my summer-long sabbatical. At the end of a box canyon along the Chama river in New Mexico, I was escorted into high-desert beauty, invited into the Benedictine prayer rhythms, and plunged into the blessed sound of silence.

While there, one of the stories I read from a book on desert wisdom was of an amma (a spiritual mother) who lived for sixty years by a river yet never once, in all that time, looked up to see the river. I'm sure the so-called wisdom of that discipline was to be singularly focused on God. But it provoked a strong protest from my soul: The river, as an aspect of God's creation, reveals God's nature. We see God through his handiwork. "The earth is the LORD's, and the fulness thereof," is how the psalmist put it.[1] To decline to observe and appreciate a river is akin to ignoring God's efforts at self-revelation. Worse, it's about as rude as refusing to make eye contact with someone when they're speaking to you.

Against such ancient desert wisdom, I've always been partial to the more modern monkish wisdom of the *liber mundi*—"the world as a book." Spiritual reading (*lectio divina*) of a book is not so much about gaining information (we've already got more than enough of that) as it is a way to pray. It's the same with creation. It's not primarily about biology or geography; it's about theology, listening to God through his handiwork. Thomas Moore writes, "The monk knows that without a constant and intimate relationship with nature, divinity is not fully revealed."[2]

With that in mind, I claim all of creation as my cell, my classroom, my playground, my sanctuary.

Grace and peace,
Pastor Eric

THE GOSPEL ACCORDING TO COUNTRY MUSIC

I will sing a new song to you, O God.
PSALM 144:9

ADMITTEDLY, I'VE NEVER been much of a fan of country music, with its twangy sound, cowboy hats, pickup trucks, and broken lives. Every song seems to be some version of "somebody done somebody wrong"; same song, next verse. Country, I long ago decided, is pathetic music for pathetic people, and I wanted nothing to do with it.

But then one day some time ago, I pushed the "scan" button on my car's FM radio. A song I had never heard before was playing, and something about it grabbed my attention. I listened to it. The lyrics, even the twang, struck a deep chord within my soul: Somebody was singing my song! I realized, with a strange mixture of sadness and humor, that my life had become an arrangement of a country song, complete with the classic themes of heartache, betrayal, and loneliness.

I was now one of those pathetic people. (I even ended up with an old Chevy pickup truck!)

The thing I've come to appreciate about country music is the ways it validates real life for real people. It acknowledges the pain and the failure which often accompany us at various points of the journey, almost normalizing it as part of the human condition. Such honesty is the prerequisite to receiving redemption. Jesus says it with brilliant simplicity: "You shall know the truth, and the truth shall set you free."[3]

In the midst of a deep personal sadness, as I was struggling to find a new song, I was given a tremendous gift. I don't even know where it came from, but it was such a strong, hopeful, and reassuring conviction that I am inclined to think it came from God. I had a clear sense that because God is a redeemer, the second half of my life would be better than the first. I didn't know exactly what that meant at the time, and I didn't know the specifics of what it would look like, but I believed it to be true nonetheless, and I resolved to do everything I could to cooperate with a redemptive outcome.

Redemption, for me, has been multifaceted and in many respects, too deep for words. But one of the magnificent ways I have experienced it is through the ways that Elizabeth and I were able to support, encourage, and care for one another during a very dark season of our lives, a season which has more recently given way to much healing, love, joy, and delight. Together, we have been ushered freshly into resurrection.

In ways that I never could have imagined, and in ways that

still seem too good to be true, I am most happy to report and to bear witness to the fact that, in the words of the psalmist, God has "put a new song in my mouth."[4]

Grace and peace,
Pastor Eric

BREATHING LESSONS

Then the LORD *God . . . breathed into his nostrils the breath of life; and the man became a living being.*
GENESIS 2:7

I feel closer to what language can't reach.
RAINER MARIA RILKE, "Moving Forward"

Enter the breathing that is more than your own.
RAINER MARIA RILKE, Part Two, Sonnet XXVII

EVERY TIME A NURSE gets ready to check my blood pressure, I ask for a few moments' pause in order to first close my eyes, go to my place of serenity, and breathe deeply. It's a meditative practice I've learned that gets the old BP at least somewhat close to a normal range and keeps the docs from throwing prescriptions at me. For a guy that usually looks pretty laid-back on the outside, I seem to be wired pretty tightly on the inside. And as we all know, mounting pressure on the inside can be dangerous; take a lesson from Kilauea, an active volcano in Hawaii. Everything and everyone needs a pressure-relief valve. Knowing this, the Designer of our lives built one in and named it "sabbath"—one day each week to take a break from work, to enjoy the gifts of the creation. To catch our breath. Additionally, every once in a while, it's good to enter an extended sabbath season.

Back in the summer of 2006, I took a three-month sabbatical, following the first eight years of this congregation's life. Those were exciting days, full of growth, ministry development, and construction projects. They were also exhausting years, and I limped into that season barely sucking air. In most ways the time away was good and restorative, and I look back on that summer of rest and exploration and reflection as a gift. But my return to work one hundred days later was pretty rocky. In fact, I almost burned up on reentry. There are probably multiple reasons for that, but one of them, I believe, was the extended time away that disrupted my weekly rhythms of worship-work-play-rest.

Hoping for a smoother transition, I asked our session if I could spread out my next sabbatical over three years, one month at a time. They agreed, and this first mini-sabbatical will be from May 28 to June 25. Here are the highlights: I'll spend eight days in Spain, walking a stretch of the Camino de Santiago with my dear friend Michael LeRoy. Later in the month, my daughter Sadie will accompany me on a trip to Princeton, where I will give a lecture on Karl Barth that my father wrote but is no longer able to deliver. In between those flying trips will be road trips with Elizabeth to places like Nelson, British Columbia; Moscow, Idaho; and Lakeside, Montana. In each case "we'll get there fast and then we'll take it slow," taking in beauty and solitude.[5] Hiking on trails. Breathing deeply.

The story is told of a South American tribe that went on a long march, day after day, when all of a sudden, they would stop walking, sit down to rest for a while, and then make camp for a couple of days before going any farther. When asked why, they explained that they needed the time of rest so that their souls could catch up with them.

As one who has been entrusted with the care of souls, I appreciate our congregation's recognition that I also need to take time to pay attention to my own soul, to attend to its needs and to honor the invitations it extends to me. It begins with the breath. "Breathe on me, breath of God."[6]

Grace and peace,
Pastor Eric

HOUND OF HEAVEN

All creatures of our God and King . . .
SAINT FRANCIS OF ASSISI

She was at first named after a stretch of the Washington coast where I caught and ate smelt for the first time. Later she was, additionally, named after the first—and for a while, the only—black child to enter an all-white school: Ruby Beach and Ruby Bridges.

As black Labrador retrievers go, she was typical: friendly, gentle, playful, insatiably hungry, and fiercely loyal. But with a strong line of English setter included in her blood, she also had tremendous hunting instincts: a keen nose, a pointer reflex, and a soft "mouth" that once snatched a grouse right out of the air and, on my command, released it unharmed.

Ruby and I entered midlife together, side-by-side, and then, as if she stepped onto one of those moving sidewalks in an airport terminal, Ruby accelerated her way far ahead of me toward old age. But she was reluctant to act her age.

Even as her body began to fail and painful joints protested, she managed to maintain a readiness—an eagerness even—for a walk in the woods where her biggest, most delicious challenge, it seemed, involved deciding which scents to follow, crisscrossing the path, nose near the ground, eyes ahead, picking up the glorious, intoxicating smells of deer, coyotes, moose, porcupines, turkeys, and heaven-knows-what-else.

My instincts, on the other hand, led me in a different direction. While Ruby darted ahead or lingered behind, depending on where the most compelling smells were, I plodded steadily along, engaged in a rhythmic discipline of what Saint Benedict called the *opus Dei*: the work of God, namely, prayer.

I recall—during a season as a young, teenage disciple—adhering to a devotional pattern prescribed for me by a mentor: a daily "quiet time" that included Scripture reading and prayer. Being a kinesthetic person, I gradually discovered that finding a way to include my body made for a more meaningful encounter with God. So over the years I've experimented with running, biking, and swimming. But I've always come back to—and now settled in on—walking.

For me, the language of prayer is most meaningfully expressed when I'm out walking. But it's even more specific than that: Connecting with God (which is, I think, what prayer is mostly about) happens best on a trail rather than a sidewalk, in nature more so than in so-called developed areas, and in solitude instead of company.

Which is why Ruby and I got along so well, I suppose.

While she followed her nose, chasing down fresh scents, terrorizing the occasional critter, I followed my heart, searching new promptings from the Spirit, attending to the demands and the invitations of my soul. On the days I didn't get a walk in, I always felt somehow less than my best self, deprived. Based on the exuberance of her tail on the day we resumed our ritual, I think Ruby may have felt the same way.

It occurs to me just now that there isn't a living creature who has overheard my most intimate prayers, spanning the broad spectrum from lamentation to praise, more than Ruby. She has heard my confessions of sin, my expressions of fear, the anguished cries of my heart, my struggles to make sense of my life, and my inarticulate attempts to return thanks to God. She has been a steady, faithful, and unorthodox (I wonder what my old mentor would say) devotional companion, sharing with me an enthusiastic love of beauty embedded in the creation. She lived her life fully and vibrantly, and in so doing, helped me to live mine, while quite differently, just so. All creatures reflect some aspect of the Creator, and Ruby, quite naturally and wonderfully, pointed me—always on the hunt for the holy—to God. In that respect, a dog named after a beach and a brave little black girl has been, for me, a canine high priest.

Grace and peace,
Pastor Eric

PUNCHED BY AN ANGEL

Jacob's hip was put out of joint as he wrestled with him.

GENESIS 32:25

As many of you well know, it was nearly seven years ago (although it now seems so much longer) that I entered a season of anguish which, even now that I am better than ever, I am not inclined to minimize. It was an experience of deep darkness and great sadness of the type that defies description. But early on, the story of Jacob wrestling an angel in the darkness became an important and potent metaphor for me. I was in the struggle of my life, and Jacob loaned me his fierce determination, a holy refusal to give up. On borrowed faith, I resolved that I would not let go until God blessed me. I am endlessly grateful for the ways God has done just that, in myriad and beautiful ways (most notably through my marriage to Elizabeth) that even now leave me amazed by grace and nearly as speechless as before.

Inexplicably, during that same time, I developed a pain in

my right hip that I have been trying to both understand and manage off and on ever since, involving a variety of medical interventions and high doses of ibuprofen. Finally, an MRI recently revealed what was really going on. The diagnosis: "Extensive degenerative maceration and tearing of the acetabular labrum." The physician's assistant who was interpreting it to me said, "Basically, you're a mess in there." The prescription: total hip arthroplasty. I need a hip replacement.

On April 13, I am scheduled for the surgery that will swap my injured hip with an impressive combination of titanium, ceramic, and polyethylene, something which—in the words of my surgeon (words which teeter on the edge of hubris)—"will be better than the original parts God gave you." Additionally, he tells me that it will involve a six-week recovery period, but that I will be able to resume my workout routine once the stitches are out. I'm happy about that, as I have a date with my daughter to climb Mount Baker together in September: a hefty and enticing rehab carrot dangling in front of me.

We accumulate reminders—some in our bodies, others in our memories—of struggles that we have endured and survived. Paul carried around a host of thorn-in-the-flesh reminders of his beatings, floggings, and of once being stoned. Even after his resurrection, Jesus retained the scars of his crucifixion; in fact, some theologians suggest that they were what caused his disciples in Emmaus to finally recognize him. And Jacob. The Contender.[7] His body a repository for the remnants of a grueling midnight wrestling match, a visceral reminder of a dark and blessed night which was evoked with every wincing step for the rest of his 147 years, hobbling around with the aid of a Canaanite cane until he was "gathered to his people, old and full of days."[8] Trophy-like, his lingering limp was the permanent physical evidence that he had striven with God and with man and lived to tell the story.

I am grateful for the technology and medical skill that makes my upcoming hip surgery possible, allowing me to resume a number of activities that have been significantly curtailed in recent years. I am grateful for good insurance that makes it affordable. And that gratitude mounts as I am persuaded that it is far quicker and easier to repair an injured hip than it is to heal a broken heart. And while I will no longer, presumably, walk with a limp, I will forever carry the scar which will keep me in struggling solidarity with Jacob, my brother and patron saint, who got punched by an angel but who didn't get knocked out.

Grace and peace,
Pastor Eric

PS—I don't believe anyone has ever written a poem for me until this month, when a dear friend sent me this hope-filled gift:

ERIC

Done with wrestling
haunting inconsequential
vestiges of the past—
turn toward Peniel
God is waiting
to strive with you;
do not let go
till you are blessed;
trouble placid
baptismal waters,
then limp away
expectantly;
you are made whole
soon enough!

SAMUEL MAHAFFY[9]

SONGS IN THE KEY OF LIFE

He taught me how to sing the latest God-song,
a praise-song to our God.
PSALM 40:3, MSG

I RECALL A SEASON OF ANGUISH about ten years ago when my life was harshly disrupted, sending me reeling into a downward spiral of depression and disorientation. From the bottom of a dark pit of despair, I recalled these hope-filled words: "We can ignore even pleasure. But pain insists upon being attended to. God whispers to us in our pleasures, speaks in our conscience, but shouts in our pains: it is His megaphone to rouse a deaf world" (C. S. Lewis).[10] Indeed, whatever hardness of heart or hearing impairment I had previously suffered pretty much went away during that time. With pleasure being a mere memory, the uninvited, unwelcome pain softened my heart and restored my hearing. I was all ears. And although I wouldn't ever send a cordial invitation to pain to come for another visit, I am grateful for the many ways it eventually ushered me into deeper intimacy with our Lord.

Months later, when hollowness finally gave way to healing, I spent some time reflecting on what I had learned. Mostly, I was pleased to conclude that everything I had believed, taught, and preached about the life of faith was true, and it held up when tested by fire. With this one exception: My understanding of the biblical notion of "abundant life" was based on the false assumption that God's desire was for me to be happy. What I came to realize is that "abundance" is meant to represent the entire spectrum of the human experience. After all, if Jesus came to bring us the fullness of life, his own life should reflect it. And the life of Jesus ranges from the horrors of the crucifixion to the glories of the resurrection. So why should it be any different for us? Jesus didn't come to deliver us from our humanity and its accompanying heartaches, but to join us in it all (the good, the bad, the beautiful, and the ugly) and to use it as the raw material to redeem our lives.

Turns out Professor Pain is a really effective teacher.

As was my professor-pastor-father. I learned a lot from him during the fifty-five years we shared life together, a lot of things for which I will always be grateful. What surprised me was what he taught me as he was dying. While his words were expectedly sparse, his joy was uncommonly present. He was calm, peaceful, serene, and "perfectly content." After a lifetime of being devoted to his Savior, he approached the end of his days fully prepared. He was ready. During his final hours, we watched and listened as he straddled that thin threshold between earth and heaven. It was Elizabeth who had the distinct honor of being with him when she heard him talking to someone on the other side of that threshold: "I'm Eugene," he said, plain as day. "Take me with you." Consequently, and now more than ever, "I believe in the resurrection of the body."[11] On the final exam of life, that's the only thing we need to get right.

In the fresh wake of grief following the death of my beloved dad, and out of my desire to experience abundant life for myself, I embrace this season of lamentation by singing the blues. Requiem is the soundtrack of my heart. I pray in D minor. But one day—I know this to be true—I will learn the latest God-song, and I will sing the Hallelujah chorus once again.

Grace and peace,
Pastor Eric

CREDO

Tell me what you know about God and
the world and the human soul.

SARA GROVES, "In the Girl There's a Room"

A HANDFUL OF THINGS (some of them surprising) that I have learned and come to believe while walking through a season of midlife:

- Orientation always gives way to Disorientation, which eventually leads to Reorientation (credit: theologian Walter Brueggemann).[12]
- Despite biblical evidence to the contrary, sometimes it is more blessed to receive than it is to give.
- Tears are too holy a thing to be attended to with cheap facial tissue. Use Puffs.
- I have some of the most amazing friends on the planet.
- I am no less a fan of marriage than ever before.

- My theology has been mightily tested and has proven to be true.
- God really does hear the cries of the brokenhearted.
- Hope is one of the most powerful forces that exists. (I think Saint Paul must have had a brain fart when listing the fruits of the Spirit in Galatians 5; he omitted hope.)
- No matter what, love is still a worthy cause (credit: musician Sara Groves).[13]
- Surrender, as a spiritual discipline, is not as much about giving up as it is about moving on (credit: Benedictine sister Joan Chittister).[14]
- There are powerful healing systems embedded throughout the created order, but they require our cooperation in order to be effective.
- Simple things are holy.
- When it comes to the reach of redemption, God has a freakishly long arm.
- The human soul needs solitude like the body needs air.
- Pain is a bellows on the fire of prayer.
- I still have a lot to learn.

Grace and peace,
Pastor Eric

2

What God Is About

REDEEMING THE RAGS

Then I lowered my head and, trembling for all that I had seen, I myself walked up to the Ragman. I told him my name with shame, for I was a sorry figure next to him. Then I took off all my clothes in that place, and I said to him with dear yearning in my voice: "Dress me."

He dressed me. My Lord, he put new rags on me, and I am a wonder beside him. The Ragman, the Ragman, the Christ!

WALTER WANGERIN, JR., *Ragman and Other Cries of Faith*

WE KNOW THIS MUCH, according to the biblical witness, although nobody really understands it: Starting from the very, very beginning, and for the first six days, God created everything *ex nihilo*—out of nothing. Creation, in the technical sense of the term, ended at sundown on day six of the world's first workweek; it was *finito*. Done. Finished. Since then all creativity has involved the rearrangement and recovery and recycling of the inchoate stuff that God called into existence at the birth of the cosmos. After a day of sabbath rest and beginning with the eighth day of history, God has been hard at work reshaping, reworking, reclaiming this stuff: earth, air, water, plants, animals, and people. The biblical enjoiner to "till and to keep" the garden is the ongoing invitation extended to the children of God to participate in the care and the enjoyment and the healing of all that is in the world. The miraculous, formative energies of Creation give way to the holy—and no less miraculous—work of redemption.

The debut of our new sanctuary banner this summer is a celebration of this redemptive reality. Scraps of fabric—which, by themselves, are not useful for much—have been gathered together from various ragbags around town and sewn together as a backdrop to the cross, the central focal point both visually and theologically to our life together. The result is a work of art which radiates beauty and hope. It's what happens whenever the cross is allowed to overshadow the listless, lifeless, and fractured parts of our lives. Redemption doesn't create something altogether new, but rather recreates something beautiful out of the tattered, worn-down, rejected, and otherwise shameful pieces of our lives.

Kaye Linda Johnson and Jonelle Bellis—our redemptive seamstresses—left the edges of the banner unhemmed, uneven because they know the truth of what the Jungian psychoanalyst James Hollis insists: namely, that life remains "raggedy and incomplete."[1] Put another way by the Catholic theologian Karl Rahner, our lives are composed of an unfinished symphony and we must learn to live with the "insufficiency of everything attainable."[2] In still other words, we will always have loose ends and frayed edges in our lives, for even the resurrected Jesus retained his scars.

Redemption, you see, is not about erasing a painful past

or waving a magic wand to make all that is wrong in our world go away. The miracle of redemption is that God gathers up the rags and tattered tales of our lives and *from that very stuff* gently pieces us back together, creating something different and beautiful and whole.

Grace and peace,
Pastor Eric

CHEW ON THIS

And she gave birth to her firstborn son and wrapped him in bands of cloth, and laid him in a manger, because there was no place for them in the inn.

LUKE 2:7

ADVENT, AS A FOUR-SUNDAY season of preparation, provides us with a two-pronged emphasis for worship and devotion. It both relives the anticipation of a world eager to welcome the Messiah two millennia ago and it invites us to anticipate his return in glory. The first coming of Christ is a historical fact. The second coming of Christ is an eschatological promise. These are the primary salvation events which bookend our present lives somewhere in between: the Incarnation and the Parousia. Simultaneously, we celebrate the former and we lean toward the latter, praying, "Thy kingdom come," all the while living in the overarching reality that God is *with* us here and now.

According to the Gospel storyteller Luke, when the angels visited the shepherds to issue their glorious, nocturnal announcement that the Savior had been born, they cited two things as signs to look for: the baby would be wrapped in bands of cloth, and he would be found lying in a manger.

That strikes me as a bit odd, at least when I think of all the other signs that could have accompanied his arrival. After all, the magi had a special star that pointed the way to Jesus. And in adulthood a large number of signs confirmed his identity as the Messiah. He turned water into wine, he calmed a storm, he multiplied loaves of bread, he fished a coin out of a smallmouth bass,[3] and he brought dead-man Lazarus back to life, to name but a few of the more impressive ones.

But for the boys and men who were keeping watch of the sheep herds on that pivotal Palestinian night, the signs were much more ordinary, everyday, unimpressive: strips of cloth swaddling a baby boy, and a manger.

Manger derives from the Latin word *mandere*, "to chew," referring, as you might easily guess, to the trough that holds feed for barnyard animals. And it was, as we correctly learned as children, the first bed in which Jesus slept. Far from the mahogany crib that my father lovingly handcrafted for my children, this thing was crude and dirty, perhaps even a bit slobbery.

This was no mistake. It was not a divine oversight that the infant-king-son-of-God-savior-of-the-world didn't have a reservation at a five-star hotel. It was quite intentional. It was a birthing that resonated with the purposes of God, who does not remain confined to the lofty places, but stoops, condescends, and enters into lives which retain many rough edges that would, by most estimations of decency, prove hostile to hosting the Holy.

Thankfully, if not miraculously, such conditions do not deter God from either coming or staying among us. He is used to roughing it. Manger accommodations will do just fine. In fact, a feed trough may be the most appropriate place to lay the head of the one who claimed to be the Bread of Life. For the world's populace, from the day he was born to the present day, has alternated between either gratefully receiving him or chewing him up and spitting him out.

Jesus began and ended his life as a homeless man. He's used to discomfort. He's accustomed to bad treatment. He has willingly assumed a nomadic existence as a sojourner with no place to call home.

But (and here is the point of it all): He is still itinerating around this old world, wandering about, seeking hospitable hearts in which to take up residence, searching out some more roughhewn people in which to dwell, these living mangers, which are our lives, where we—slobber and all—welcome the Life of God to abide and to reign.

Grace and peace,
Pastor Eric

COME AGAIN?

So Christ, having been offered once to bear the sins of many, will appear a second time, not to deal with sin, but to save those who are eagerly waiting for him.
HEBREWS 9:28

THE FUTURE, UNCERTAIN as it insists on being, is the source of both endless anxiety and boundless curiosity. Most people are fascinated with the future, eager to know what is to come, interested in knowing what awaits them, so they know how to prepare for whatever lies ahead. This intrigue is what keeps in business those so-called diviners who read palms, those who peer into crystal balls, and those who interpret tarot cards. Somewhat more legitimate are the people whose jobs are to pay attention to trends, sometimes forecasting the weather by using computer models, other times using sophisticated algorithms to anticipate where things are heading, from stock values to consumer-spending patterns to climate change.

People—prone as they are to paying attention to patterns

because of the ways our brains are wired—will actually "see" patterns where none exist. So greedy are we to anticipate the future that we will, in other words, fabricate predictive patterns even within truly random arenas. While it appears that this is a survival skill that has evolved in certain species (let's stick with *homo sapiens* for now), it can sometimes get us into trouble, as when, for example, we make decisions in the present based on erroneous assumptions about the future.

Futurists are people who pay attention to the signs of today which are serving as pointers to help predict the future, in order to help us make appropriate decisions in the present. Some futurists are more legitimate than others, based largely on the information being used. Others seem to be based more on myth and fear. For example, predictions about the world's end, based on the Mayan calendar, were groundless: We all woke up last December 22, 2012, to the realization that we had not been obliterated by a meteor after all.[4] Y2K was a nonevent, save for all the food and water that was hoarded in late 1999.[5]

Even one of the popes (Sylvester II) tried his hand at divining, saying that the world as we know it would close at the end of the Christian millennium with the return of Jesus on January 1, 1000. Not to be outdone, Pope Innocent III predicted that the world would end 666 years after the rise of Islam. Even so great a mind as the Protestant reformer Martin Luther took a shot at it, but he was off by over four hundred years . . . and counting. But Harold Camping gets the award for most perseverant prognosticator, making no fewer than five public predictions for the world's end. And yet, here we are. (Although I've lost track of where *he* is.)[6]

God's promises are typically accompanied by signs; call them *promisigns*, if you like. For Adam the promisign was a tree. For Noah it was a rainbow. Moses received the twin tablets, Abraham was circumcised, and David got a throne. In each case, these were the signs that accompanied the promise of God's covenant. When God (through an angel) announced the arrival of the Savior of the world, the shepherds were assured of the veracity of the promise through this sign: "You will find a child wrapped in bands of cloth and lying in a manger."[7]

That child grew up and performed a slew of signs and wonders, which further verified his messianic identity: healing, feeding, resurrecting, calming, etc. But the enduring signs he left us amount to a simple yet sacred trinity of signs: water, bread, wine. These are the promisigns of his abiding presence with us, located at a font and a table, until he returns on a cloud and sits us down to a feast.

That "until" can be a tricky place in which to live, this ever-expanding time between the first and the second comings of Christ. The weeks of Advent teach us how to live in the gap, inviting us to embrace the promisign of the Savior of the world who came, who comes, and who will come again, living in the *now* and the *not yet* of God's presence and God's promises, leaning into that day when there will be a magnificent marriage of heaven and earth, a united Kingdom of God, the long-awaited Day of the Lord, when Jesus, in all his saving glory, comes again. Just as he promised.

Grace and peace,
Pastor Eric

ADVENT-AGEOUS

Come, thou long-expected Jesus . . .

CHARLES WESLEY, "Come, Thou Long-Expected Jesus"

THE GOOD NEWS STORY—*the Kingdom of God is at hand!*—must be re-storied in every season and in every person. As each one of us becomes a fresh incarnation of Jesus, the church gradually, generationally reaches its full stature. The second advent, or the return of Christ, happens through each of us as we heed John the Baptist's invitation to turn from our sin and re-turn to our Maker. Or, said another way, to join Nicodemus in being "born again."[8] The advantage of Advent is in its summons to begin again. If that sounds difficult, you heard right.

When we consider the Incarnation—the way that God personally showed up in the world—we see humility and simplicity and poverty. And so if we understand today's church as the present manifestation of the body of Christ (which, indeed it is) then it must, I'm convinced, reflect the *way* God came to us in Jesus. Over and against the prevailing view that the church should offer a compelling demonstration of the *power* of God, and therefore should use the means and methods that would reflect that might and that effectiveness, God's way is a lowly way: coming to us in the form of a newborn, blessing meekness, embodying servanthood, affirming humility. If we are going to be a people born of Jesus, we are going to need to get in touch with our poverty. And rather than operating out of a posture of strength and resources, we'll need instead to work from a position of weakness: the precise environment in which divine strength is perfected. The apostle Paul put it this way: "Let the same mind be in you that was in Christ Jesus, who, though he was in the form of God, did not regard equality with God as something to be exploited, but emptied himself, taking the form of a slave, being born in human likeness. And being found in human form, he humbled himself and became obedient to the point of death—even death on a cross."[9]

I'll be the first to admit that this may not sound like the American way, and it may not even feel like the natural way. But it is, nonetheless, the Jesus way. It is a way that embraces the "now-but-not-yet" ambiguities of Advent, as it holds us in the midst of life's uncertainties, along with all that remains incomplete, inviting us, Mary-like, to ponder all these things in our hearts.[10]

The pendulum of Advent typically swings between the celebration of the *birth* of Jesus (when God became one of us), and the anticipation of Christ's *return* in glory. But those past and future bookends in the salvation story—both Incarnation and Parousia—reflect, above all, the gift of divine *Presence*. This Advent I hope that we can, while not forgetting the past nor neglecting the future, remain in the present by practicing the Presence. The Return of Christ happens in each one of us as we create hospitable environments for the Spirit of Christ to indwell. "Come, thou long-expected Jesus . . . born to reign *in us* forever."[11]

Grace and peace,
Pastor Eric

MAKING A LIST

If you conquer, you will be clothed like them in white robes, and I will not blot your name out of the book of life.

REVELATION 3:5

I'M A LIST-MAKER. It's one of the ways I organize my days: by writing down the tasks that I want to accomplish. Not having a supervisor, and being self-directed, it's one of the ways I try to manage the gift of freedom and responsibility that comes with this blessed vocation, by identifying work that I believe is of greatest importance. Along with the vocational freedom associated with this calling comes the ability to squander it, and so my lists keep me on track and accountable, so I don't fritter away my time.

Moreover, I'm finding that my memory is not what it once was, and I'm prone to forget. If I add them to my list as the ideas and plans come to mind, I'm less likely to let things slip by, only to have them jolt me awake in the middle of the night when they inconveniently sneak back into my consciousness.

But (and here's a confession) perhaps the biggest reason I make up my daily to-do list is that it gives me a sense of accomplishment. When I head home at the end of a day and see all of those beautiful lines crossing off my self-imposed assignments, it gives me a sense of satisfaction, like I did something worthwhile that day. I justified my existence and my salary. And I can go home feeling good about myself. Again, I'm not proud to admit this, as it reveals the vestiges of a works-righteousness ethic within me that refuses to die.

The week that I spent on the Camino de Santiago in Spain earlier this summer gave me a blessed respite from my addiction to lists. On the Camino, there is only one essential task: walk. The only thing to accomplish each day is to get from one town to the next. That's the sole goal: put one foot in front of the other and repeat this two-step pattern for eighteen miles or so. Don't return emails or phone calls or library books. Don't write a sermon. Don't get a haircut. Just walk. Having that as the one task to accomplish every day was accompanied by a profound sense of spaciousness that allowed me to have what is for me the rare experience of "clearing my mind." Taking a sabbatical from lists was good for me.

I take some comfort in seeing that God is also a list-maker.

However, God's lists are not composed of tasks to be done, or reminders due to forgetfulness, or a device for tracking accomplishments in order to feel good about Godself. Rather, God's lists are comprised of the personal names of his children, recorded in the Lamb's Book of Life. God, I believe, delights in listing the names of the baptized in his book. And since they are inscribed with indelible ink, he wouldn't even think about crossing any of them off. Because it's not a to-do list. It's a to-die-for list. For God so loves the world.

Grace and peace,
Pastor Eric

ANGELS WE HAVE HEARD . . . AND HIJACKED

Are not all angels spirits in the divine service, sent to serve for the sake of those who are to inherit salvation?

HEBREWS 1:14

ARE THERE ANGELS among us? If so, where are they, and what in the world are they doing? Whoever and wherever they are, they certainly show up in our language a lot. For example, people who escape an accident without serious injuries will often credit "a guardian angel watching over me." An especially well-behaved child might get referred to as "a perfect angel," and someone who sings beautifully is said to have "the voice of an angel."

A cursory study of art history will reveal that we've always been fascinated by angels, especially as they are portrayed in the Scriptures. But in our day the interest has gone viral and has spilled imaginatively well beyond the borders of the Bible. Type the word *angel* into a search engine and you'll come up with over three billion results. As a point of comparison, that's nine times more results than what you'd get if you entered the now trendy word *zombie*. It appears that angels, for all their shy tendencies, are only growing in popularity.

The American sociologist Robert Wuthnow, writing in 1998, traces our increasing fascination over the last quarter century:

> Overall, the number of books on angels (according to the Library of Congress) rose from 20 published between 1971 and 1975, to 31 between 1976 and 1980, 34 between 1981 and 1985, 57 between 1986 and 1990, and 110 between 1991 and 1995. During the last of these periods, total sales of angel books were estimated to exceed five million copies.[12]

And then there's the plethora of movies and television shows, from *Angels in America* to *Touched by an Angel*, that have flooded screens both big and small. It's little wonder that then–First Lady Hillary Clinton declared 1995 the Year of the Angel.

For all of the interest they get, angels are also victim to much misinformation and misrepresentation. Because I believe we are called to be people of the truth, I get concerned when, at times of death, I hear erroneous comments from survivors about "now having an angel to watch over me." But grief is not the time to correct anybody's unorthodox views on angelology, so I'm doing it now. While such sentiments may provide comfort or be offered as a source of consolation to grieving people, they are not grounded in any semblance of biblical truth and are, therefore, nothing more than false hope. Lies, really. Dead children aren't transformed into angels. People don't die and then become our guardian angels. That's baloney.

Rather, angels are spiritual beings created by God for specific purposes, primarily as messengers, but also to provide aid and protection to people in need. They are real and they are operative in our world, functioning as agents of God's will in a variety of ways. So don't be surprised (or afraid) if you meet one. Practice hospitality to a stranger, and you might just find yourself entertaining one.[13] But please don't ascribe such an identity to mere mortals, no matter how angelic you consider them to be. At the time of death we don't become angels; we inherit resurrection. And that is far and away better.

Grace and peace,
Pastor Eric

EUCATASTROPHE

We know that all things work together for good for those who love God, who are called according to his purpose.

ROMANS 8:28

IT MAY BE THE QUESTION that has been asked more than any other one throughout the history of the world: *If God really is so good and so powerful, why do bad things happen to people—good and bad alike?* The question has prompted endless theories, none of them, to my way of thinking, providing satisfactory answers.

If there was only one thing to be learned from the Incarnation, it would be to establish the experience of suffering as normative, both for God and for humanity. Jesus' suffering demonstrates that God, rather than eradicating it from the human scene, participates in our suffering, making it meaningful, employing it as a divine agent for godly ends.

Suffering is the furnace that forges the soul for holiness. In fact, some of the holy ones claim that it's impossible to grow into Christlikeness without the experience of suffering, whether personally or vicariously. It is the unwelcome yet necessary tool in the workshop of God's love that re-forms us in the *imago Dei*. Asking why suffering exists in this world is like asking why $A = \pi r^2$ or why we have ten fingers (why not twelve?) or why cottonwood-tree leaves give off the most delicious scent in spring. We may not understand precisely why any of those things exist, but like suffering, they are among the universal laws of the world in which we live.

Which is why people of faith tend to ask the age-old question a little differently, looking for the ways in which God is present to us in our suffering. Saint Paul, although he suffered severe anguish, didn't even bother to ask the question, turning it instead into a statement of faith, insisting that God works all things together for good, or what J. R. R. Tolkien called *eucatastrophe*: a sudden and favorable resolution of events in a story; a happy ending.[14]

That little prefix *eu* has the power to turn a word favorably on its ear. It's what makes a word good (eulogy), a discovery glad (Eureka!), a feeling glorious (euphoria), a sound pleasing (euphonious). It's what transforms a meal into a sacrament (Eucharist), and what makes the gospel truly good news (*euangelion*/evangelism). But it doesn't just change words; it changes stories. It is the easy-to-miss gift which God brings to the table, to the world, to our lives, so that when all other signs point to failure or tragedy, the Good-Word (Eu-Logos) companions us, causing new life to emerge from otherwise dismal circumstances.

The Incarnation, far surpassing the sweet images of

no-crying-he-makes-baby-Jesus, celebrates the unique ways that God continues to do some of his very best work in the darkest, hardest, and most painful and bewildering circumstances of our lives. But there are no shortcuts. There were none for the Son of God, and there aren't any for the sons and daughters of God either.

This morning, I read a story about a father who took his son to Drew University to register him for college. He said to the dean of admissions, "This is a smart kid. Why will it take four years? Can't you do it in two?" The dean, who was a gardener, said, "It takes four years to make an educated person. It takes two years to make zucchini. Which do you want?"

It takes a long time to make a disciple. It takes a lifetime to complete a baptism.

Those who do not know the eucatastrophic truth of Romans 8 may have simply not remained in the crucible long enough to experience the fecundity of it. Redemption takes time. And while, like a garden, it may at times appear latent, it is always and everywhere working, never sleeping, effecting goodly outcomes in the very worst of times. Deeply, covertly, slowly, surely, redemption is making its way. Wait for it. Chances are good—very good—that your waiting will eventually escort you into the surprise of a happy ending.

Grace and peace,
Pastor Eric

PLACE OF REFUGE

Happy are all who take refuge in him.
PSALM 2:12

INITIALLY PROMPTED by promises of good snorkeling, one of the destinations during our recent family vacation to Hawaii was a most amazing spot known as Pu'uhonua O Hōnaunau. Translation: "Place of Refuge."

The ancient Hawaiians, you could say, were a thoroughly religious people. Polytheistic in practice, they were immersed in a belief system that their world was dominated and controlled by a wide variety of gods. Such beliefs led them to develop a highly sophisticated set of religious laws for the purpose of guiding lifestyle choices and keeping the gods' wrath at bay, as well as outlining punishments suitable for any number of crimes.

For example, being a sexist society, men and women were not permitted to eat together. And being a class society, those of lower classes weren't allowed to even set foot on the trails traveled by upper classes. Ordinary citizens, moreover, were forbidden to approach a chief, so as not to allow their lower-class shadows to be cast on him. In short, it was a society governed by *kapu*. Translation: rules, rules, and more rules.

The punishment for breaking a *kapu* does not appear to have been graduated. That is to say, minor offenses carried the same penalty as major crimes. If a woman took a bite of pork or ate a banana, she would receive the same sentence as the man who interrupted a chief who was speaking, namely, the judgment of death, and that usually by strangulation, club, or fire. For particularly heinous crimes, the sentence might be extended to the offender's entire family. Harsh as it sounds, it was, nonetheless, effective in keeping order. Additionally, it was a practice believed to avert the wrath of the gods, who might otherwise issue their own judgment in the form of earthquakes, tsunamis, or lava flows to castigate the entire community.

There was, however, one provision built into the penal system as a kind of "get out of jail free" card. If the offender of a *kapu* was quick enough to elude his would-be executioners, he could run and swim his way to Pu'uhonua—the place of refuge—where he was granted immunity. By performing certain acts of penance, the priest would then declare the person forgiven, and he could return to the community as if nothing had ever happened.

Believers in and followers of the triune God have such a place characterized by safety, forgiveness, and salvation. It's a place where life sentences are commuted in favor of eternal life, and where we hear the declaration from the High Priest that we are being sought no longer for punishment but for love and for life. That place is, of course, the cross of Jesus Christ.

The main difference between God's way and the ancient Hawaiian way is that Jesus went to the cross on *our* behalf; all we have to do is make our way to *him*. In baptism we have crossed the waters toward salvation, delivering us from certain death to new life, marking us as God's own forever, and making us heirs to the Kingdom of God. It's a gift offered not just to the fit and the lucky but to all who hobble the holy way to Christ crucified and resurrected. As we sing in worship,

I know a place, a wonderful place,
Where accused and condemned find mercy and grace.
Where the wrongs we have done, and the wrongs done to us,
Are nailed there with him, there on the cross.[15]

Let us, therefore, flee from sin and evil and find our true home at such a place of refuge from which issues a sure and certain statement: "There is therefore now no condemnation for those who are in Christ Jesus."[16]

Grace and peace,
Pastor Eric

NESTING INSTINCT

How often have I desired to gather your children together as a hen gathers her brood under her wings . . .

JESUS in Luke 13:34

I HAD READ ABOUT IT in the book *What to Expect When You're Expecting* at the same time that I was working my way through thick volumes of theology and church history sixteen years ago, just before our son, Drew, was born. It was an intense year of both theological and prenatal education—disciplines which, as I discovered, have a good deal in common with one another.

The word I was introduced to in the midst of my Fatherhood 101 education was *nesting*. It's a phenomenon which refers to the work of expectant birds who build a nest in which to lay and hatch eggs and in which baby birds are cared for until the time is right for "flight training." The nest, for birds, starts out as a home, and eventually becomes a launch pad.

Nesting is the same word used to describe the nearly

universal tendency of a mother-to-be to get her house ready to receive a new child. The nesting instinct of women causes them to do such things as to clean the house, knit baby clothes, and set up a nursery. Sometimes even unwittingly, pregnant women can be found painting the spare bedroom in unconscious preparation for the new arrival. It is a powerful and primarily maternal instinct, although it has its masculine variations as well.

The old Latin word for nest is *nidus*, referring to an origin of change, a breeding ground for new ideas, a place of grief and joy, a source of support and sharing. It's a word you won't typically hear in casual conversation, but it's the best one to describe the gathering that takes place every Sunday morning.

Worship is the experience of being nestled in the safe presence of the God of love, of being fed on the Word, and of being trained as followers of Christ. It is a fertile environment for birth and of life: new creation. It is a place where we can come just as we are and know that we will be loved and cared for much like a nursing mother nurtures her children.

But when God gathers us in the *nidus* of his love, he doesn't let us linger there for long. When the time is right—and quite often, long before we feel ready—he gives us our own version of flight training, by commissioning us as agents of his mission, sending us into the world to share the gospel, to baptize in the name of the triune God, and to teach others the ways of God. Worship, like a bird's nest, is a place for gathering and a place of scattering. It's a place to rest, and it's a place from which to take a flying leap.

In the next several weeks we will be sending people out of the *nidus* known as Colbert Presbyterian Church. Some of them are graduating from high school or college, while others will be commissioned as missionaries to serve God in other parts of the world. It's always hard to say farewell to such friends. But it's all a part of growing up and of being a faithful church—a nurturing home and a missional launch pad.

Grace and peace,
Pastor Eric

FOOLS FOR CHRIST

For ye suffer fools gladly, seeing ye yourselves are wise.
2 CORINTHIANS 11:19, KJV

WHEN WE HEAR OF SOMEONE who doesn't "suffer fools gladly," we know this to be a person who, in all likelihood, is highly intelligent and competent but who doesn't have much patience for people who are not. The phrase originates in one of Saint Paul's more sarcastic moments during his correspondence with the Corinthian congregation in first-century Greece, during a boasting contest, but has since taken on a different meaning in popular parlance. Today, a person who *suffers fools gladly* is considered virtuous for their humility and forbearance toward someone with less capacity.

However, it's one thing to graciously tolerate ignorant or incompetent people. It's quite another matter to be considered such a person oneself. And yet the apostle suggests that people who live the gospel way may be viewed by others as anything from odd to just plain stupid. "We are fools [Greek: *morons*] for the sake of Christ."[17] Why would someone choose that way?

Peter led the way and then took it to an extreme. Recall the day when Peter stepped over the gunwales of a boat to take a walk on the water during a fierce storm simply because Jesus told him to. And even though he managed to stay afloat for a few steps before he started sinking, you just know his friends—hanging on for dear life—were confirmed in their belief that the old salt wasn't the brightest candle in the barn. Who does that? What a fool.

James and John went that way as well. The two fishermen brothers, mending their nets one day, were called by Jesus to follow him, and they didn't even hesitate: They left their boat, left their dad—left *everything*—and followed Jesus for the next three years. I'd pay money to know how Zebedee reacted to their decision as the sight of them faded into the Galilean horizon, but in my imagination, he's shaking his head sadly, muttering to himself, "And to see now that their mother and I raised a couple of fools!"

Because it's good news from another world, the gospel often sounds strange to our ears. Which means that—for people who are committed to speaking the gospel truth—chances are good that they're going to come off sounding a bit foolish. ("For those who want to save their life will lose it, and those who lose their life for my sake will find it.")[18] It also means that people who *live* the gospel way are more likely to behave in unusual ways. In the great persecutions that dominated the first two centuries of the Christian era, many believers chose to suffer torture and death rather than recant their faith in Jesus. What morons.

Jesus has a way of inverting our assumptions so that what we thought was wise and good is actually foolish, and what we deemed to be dumb becomes God's chosen way for ushering in the new age. Perhaps we would do well to step out of the conventional forms of Christianity that are widely respected in social circles and do something a little crazy. For some people, that might mean a change in jobs that results in more meaningful work for less pay. For others, it might mean choosing to be with vulnerable rather than powerful people. Whatever it looks like, it's a lifestyle not likely to be emulated among most Fortune 500 employees. God's ways are not our ways, so when we follow God's ways, we run the risk of being ridiculed. What a clown.

Later this month we will, in our various ways, observe the resurrection of our Lord. Through worship and with feasting, we celebrate Easter as the great punch line to Good Friday:

> "April fools—he's not dead at all but alive and quite well!"

Lucky for us, Jesus not only suffered the ravages of the cross, but he suffers us as well. That he still—all these years later—does it *gladly* is a staggering demonstration of divine love.

Grace and peace,
Pastor Eric

3

What the Church Is About

THE OLD CHURCH BELL

Men's death I tell by doleful knell;
Lightning and thunder I break asunder;
On Sabbath all to church I call;
The sleepy head I rouse from bed;
The tempest's rage I do assuage;
When cometh harm, I sound alarm.

ANONYMOUS

THIS INSCRIPTION, FOUND on an old church bell in England, summarizes the function of bells throughout Christendom. They would be tolled whenever someone died—usually one peal for every year of life. It was also believed that they had the power to ward off fierce thunderstorms. Additionally, they were rung to summon people to worship on Sunday morning. And in the days before clocks were in use, they helped keep track of time by waking people up, marking the noon hour, and signaling the end of the workday. And finally, they would be clanged wildly to alert townspeople to danger.

The bell we have at Colbert is actually a historic church bell given to us as a gift from the Presbyterian church in Craigmont, Idaho, where it was no longer being used. This 800-pound cast-iron bell, forged many years ago in a foundry back East, was installed in a specially engineered tower and recommissioned for similar uses to its cousins of old. Of course, we don't have the same superstitious worldview today that our ancestors did, so we don't believe that the sound of bells has the power to fend off storms, and we have more modern ways for emergency communication. But otherwise, the function of an old church bell—which some traditions trace back to the fifth-century Italian Bishop Paulinus—remains intact.[1]

Every Sunday morning, at the appointed hour of worship, the bell is jerked awake by the tug of a rope. Rocking back and forth on its yoke, startling the ears (the primary receptacle for faith),[2] interrupting lingering conversations, quickening parking-lot tardies, it calls people to enter the house of the Lord, summoning the community to obey God's gift-commandment to "remember the sabbath day, and keep it holy."[3] People who live several miles from the church have told me that when the weather is right, they can hear the bell from their homes. It is one of the most primitive forms of communication, and as a connection to our ancient past, it remains the most basic summons to turn to the living God. Call to worship.

A different, smaller bell, shaped like a bowl, is struck three times at the beginning and the end of our monthly prayer services—a kind of Trinitarian signal for the beginning and the ending of our prayerful encounter with God. But whatever form it takes, the sound of a bell is a signal to turn our attention Godward. It's an invitation to prayer.

Similar to today's opening verse, another ancient bell—this one in the land of the Celts—contains the anthropomorphic testimony of its function. Even if you don't know Latin, it's best to read it aloud:

> *Funera plango, fulmina frango, sabbata pango*
> *Excito lentos, dissipo ventos, paco cruentos.*

> At obsequies I mourn, the thunderbolts I scatter, I ring in the sabbaths,
> I hustle the sluggards, I drive away storms, I proclaim peace after bloodshed.[4]

Even without such an inscription, the old bell at Colbert Presbyterian Church will continue to be rung every Sunday morning, calling us to worship—the most important activity of our week. It will continue to mark and mourn the passing of our lives as, one by one, we become heirs to Resurrection life. It will lend its festive tones to couples on their wedding day, celebrating the beginning of their covenant life together. And it will ring out the glad tidings on Christmas that Jesus Christ is born and is with us forevermore. Pray with me that one day soon it will also proclaim peace following far too much bloodshed.

Grace and peace,
Pastor Eric

FOR SEASONS

For everything there is a season,
and a time for every matter under heaven.
ECCLESIASTES 3:1

I'M WRITING THIS on the first day of fall. Known as the autumnal equinox, it is one of two days in the year when the sun shines directly over the equator, making day and night equally balanced to twelve hours each all over the world. Presumably, you're reading this on a day that is now slightly dominated by night time, as the earth and all of its occupants in the Northern Hemisphere tilt steadily toward winter.

I love living in climes that include four distinct seasons. I like the regular, rhythmical patterns of the ever-changing seasons, and I like the fact that I pretty much know what to expect from each of them. Sure, there are the occasional freak storms and crazy extreme temperatures; foul weather ebbs and flows like the tides. Additionally, the darker times of the year can afflict us with some degree of seasonal affective disorder. But mostly each season returns with its own comforting familiarity. By the way, don't ask me my preference; my favorite is (most) always the one I'm presently in.

Similarly, the church has predictable rhythms of its own. Dominated by the periods of Advent through Christmas, Lent through Easter, Pentecost, and Ordinary Time, the liturgical seasons invite us to attend to the cycles of life, death, resurrection, and return, which are instrumental in forming us for a life in Christ.

But there are other so-called seasons in our life together which, while normal, are neither predictable nor enjoyable. Presently we in the CPC faith community are living through a season that is largely punctuated by loss. Not only did we bury three of our members this summer, but we have also said goodbye to a number of people who, for various reasons, have left our church. It is a season, in other words, that is accompanied by grief and change and uncertainty about the future. The word itself comes from the Old French word, *seison*, referring to "a time of sowing," leaving me to wonder what kinds of seeds are being planted among us during this season of our life together.

As it turns out (we know this from the Scriptures, as well as through personal experience), these are times when God has a way of getting our attention, ushering us into places of humility, prayer, and discernment. They can be helpful as times of clarification and correction, as well as confirmation. And they are often the environments in which God does some of his very best work in transforming us more fully into the beloved community known as the church of Jesus Christ.

Even grief can be the *seasoning* that helps to bring out the "God-flavors of this earth."[5]

Meteorological seasons are determined by the relationship between the earth and the sun.

Ecclesiological seasons are determined by the relationship between the church and the Son.

The triune God whom we worship and serve is, alone, the same yesterday, today, and tomorrow,[6] in and out of whatever season we happen to find ourselves.

Grace and peace,
Pastor Eric

VIGIL

Discipline yourselves, keep alert.
1 PETER 5:8

I FIRST BECAME AWARE of the phenomenon long before I knew there was a name for it. Back in my preseminary days, I was a carpenter, and an interest I had in historic buildings led to a subscription to the magazine *Old House Journal*, which in turn introduced me to (among lots of other really cool things) the mansard-style roof, common in houses that were influenced by seventeenth-century French architecture. Soon thereafter, while attending seminary back East, I began to notice how prevalent the mansard roof was; many of the historical buildings sported one.

Something similar happened again a few years later with the word *vitriolic*. I came across it while reading a social-commentary piece one afternoon in the *New Yorker* and had to look up the word in the dictionary to learn that it meant "caustic" or "scathing." Since then it seems that I see and hear it with much more frequency than before. I wonder how I missed it for so long.

Hardly anybody is putting new mansard roofs on houses any longer, and yet it suddenly seemed like the greater Princeton area was flush with them. And I'm pretty sure *vitriolic* hasn't made a dramatic rise in popularity in our English lexicon. So what's going on? Why, once I was introduced to something new, did it seem to start appearing all over the place?

The name for this, I have recently discovered, is the Baader-Meinhof phenomenon. It refers to that almost universal experience when you come upon some obscure piece of information—often an unfamiliar word or name—and soon afterwards, you encounter the same subject again, often repeatedly.

The reason for this is our brains' inclination for patterns. From our earliest days as children, our brains have been undergoing a process of hard-wiring patterns, also known as "mapping," so that we can learn how to deal more efficiently with common experiences and react without having to give them much thought; it's a bit like taking a shortcut. And since we are so good at recognizing patterns, we take special notice when they occur; it becomes information that cuts to the front of the line of our conscious awareness, causing us to notice things that have been there all along. And because patterns are habit-forming, the more we are exposed to certain things, the more likely we are to notice them in other contexts.

Lord's Day worship, I believe, involves the Baader-Meinhof phenomenon inasmuch as it is introducing us to the language of faith, shaping our worldview with a distinctively Christian lens, and conditioning us to see the holy in all things and in all people.

As a result of the conditioning, we are more likely to be aware of and to experience the presence and activity of God the other six days of the week. Some people refer to these as "God-sightings." Based on Baader-Meinhof, I'm inclined to believe that for those of us who have such God-sightings, it's not that God is more present but that we have become more aware of God's presence. We are simply more alert to the prevailing rhythms of redemption.

Through weekly worship we are establishing patterns which become holy habits. We are training our brains and sensitizing our souls to be on the lookout for the sacred. God is always everywhere but is sometimes overlooked.

Pay attention.

Grace and peace,
Pastor Eric

THE WAY IS MADE BY WALKING

Teach them the good way in which they should walk.
1 KINGS 8:36; 2 CHRONICLES 6:27

THERE IS A TRAIL that meanders through the woods behind my house. It exists because, over the course of the last twenty years, I have walked the same way, creating a path. Day after day, in season and out, I have spent my mornings following what I have christened *Moose Trail,* in honor of an enormous bull I encountered one day, many years ago. Over time, the accumulation of many steps has forged a path in the woods. Walking has created the way.

If you were to catch a peek of me on one of these mornings, it wouldn't look like much. Just a middle-aged man walking slowly, sipping strong, black coffee, stopping for the occasional grouse that I've inadvertently flushed, startling me from my thoughts. Otherwise, I'm in some unimpressive rhythm of seeing what I can see, paying attention to my life, listening for God.

Some people may look at that ritualistic pattern and say, "How boring! Why don't you try something new? Go off trail! Adventure out! Bushwhack a little, for crying out loud!" But when you don't have to pay attention to route-finding, when you don't have to think about where to place your next step, something beautiful happens: When the mind doesn't have to work so hard, the soul is free to play.

I've also noticed that when I neglect my morning liturgy for a period of time, the path—with startling rapidity—becomes overtaken. Weeds and brush move in, obfuscating the path. Upon my eventual return, I have to pay closer attention to where I'm going, where I'm stepping, so that I don't stumble or lose my way.

This is the genius and the gift of Christian liturgy: The weekly patterns of divine worship establish a path that leads us Godward. We sing our songs, we say our prayers, we attend the Scriptures, and we celebrate the sacraments. These patterns, over time, form us more fully as citizens in the Kingdom of God. They establish us in the path of righteousness. They groove us in the way of godliness.

In the way that is known as the Jesus way, there are spiritual practices that form us for life in the Kingdom of God. The rhythms of worship, involving the week-after-week gathering of the people of God, I am persuaded, are essential for ushering us further down the way known as the Jesus way. It's a well-worn path, created by the movements of centuries of pilgrims, leading us into the very presence of the one revealed to us and known to us as the way, the truth, the life.[7]

The Sundays accumulate. They add up. They create grooves in the soul for the Holy Spirit to inhabit. Therefore, let us discipline ourselves to remain steady and steadfast on this pilgrim journey, lest we lose our way.

Grace and peace,
Pastor Eric

WATCH YOUR STEP

Stand at the crossroads, and look,
and ask for the ancient paths,
where the good way lies; and walk in it,
and find rest for your souls.
JEREMIAH 6:16

UNLIKE A LOT OF THINGS, there is one practice that can't be rushed. We can live on fast food, work on fast computers, and drive fast cars. We can communicate with one another instantly, hurry through our chores, and even blast through a book by speed-reading. In fact, we're getting better at it all the time as we learn more efficient ways of getting from "here" to "there" (in both the literal and the figurative sense of those words). We live on a planet that spins at the astonishing speed of one thousand miles per hour, and at times it seems that we're doing everything we can to catch up. But some things can't, by design, be rushed.

Prayer is the one thing that invites us to slow down our hearts and minds and bodies to a pace that allows us to enter a kind of holy leisure where we can be still and know God. It is one of the few things that refuses to bow to the gods of efficiency, results, or performance. There is no app for prayer (actually and unfortunately, there is; I urge you not to download it). But there are ways to train us in the art of slow prayer.

Labyrinths are among those ancient-future tools that have helped Christians do just that. They are the speed bumps of prayer, slowing us down through the circuitry of meandering pathways, leading us—pilgrim-like—on a unique journey to Christ at the center. Our newly installed labyrinth represents an invitation to decelerate life by taking a slow, prayerful walk, mindful of each and every step, attentive to every breath and nudge of the Spirit. It's an invitation to take the long way home to the one who knows no shortcuts, because while the shortest path between two points is a straight line, the journey of discipleship is a call to go the distance.

Betty Stratton, one of the key founders of this church, laid a foundation of prayer for our corporate life and ministry. She literally brought us to our knees, calling us to seek God's direction for our nascent congregation. The development of our church took longer than anyone expected, and that, it turned out, was a good thing. I regularly give thanks to God for this godly woman and her crucial role in the formation of our church. Because of her influence and enduring legacy, I am pleased to say that we now have the Betty Stratton Prayer Labyrinth. Pray it well. Watch your step. Take it slow.

Grace and peace,
Pastor Eric

TRUE CHOIR

I believe in the communion of saints . . .
THE APOSTLES' CREED

On that glad day when our friend Ben Brody joined the staff of Colbert Presbyterian Church to be our director of music ministry, I remember thinking how nice it would be to finally have a choir. Like many of you, I grew up in a church that featured organ music accompanying the great hymns of the church and a choir that sang a weekly anthem. When Colbert got its start in 1997, some of us had to get used to worship without an organ, and our attempts at developing a choir in subsequent years were spotty. With Ben on the job, along with his freshly-minted doctorate in choral conducting, I was sure we would develop a choir. It was not the first (nor the last) time that I've been wrong.

What we gradually became convinced of together is the importance of emphasizing *congregational* singing. Because we believe the rhythms of liturgy, prayer, and singing to be among the formative practices that significantly shape our identity as the children of God, finding ways to more fully engage people in worship is a priority. Since our goal is to *incarnate* the faith in a vibrant, meaningful way, we must involve our minds, bodies, and voices in that lifelong journey of becoming like Christ.

The Reformed tradition, with its emphasis on the priesthood of all believers, has always sought to demolish the artificial dividing wall between so-called priests and so-called laity. By extension, Reformed people are on guard against such designations as "expert" and "amateur" when it comes to honoring one's baptism. When we recite that line of the creed "I believe in the communion of saints," we are affirming a faith that is *historical*, *global*, and *eschatological*. Permit me to add a little flesh to these bones.

Historical: Ours is a faith that goes all the way back to "in the beginning . . ." Since that time, the people of God have composed hymns, psalms, and spiritual songs that capture their experience and understanding of living in covenant relationship with God. With the passing of centuries, some of the language can, at times, sound a bit antiquated to our ears (e.g., "Nought be all else to me, save that thou art"),[8] yet we retain it as a way of honoring our spiritual fathers and mothers, in recognition that faith is an inheritance from one generation to the next.

Global: Because of our proclivity toward parochialism, it is also helpful to be reminded that the way Christianity is practiced varies widely among various cultures. The Bible wasn't written in English, and Jesus wasn't born anywhere near North America. Singing songs in other languages ushers us into solidarity with Christians from around the world. Celebrating the unity that makes up our "one faith, one Spirit, one baptism, and one Lord" is not dependent on homogeneity (or even similarity) of language, ethnicity, or any number of cultural customs.[9]

Eschatological: The Revelation to John, our chief apocalyptic book in the Bible, provides a glimpse into the future. What was revealed to John, however, was not limited to his vision; he also heard things. And what he heard was music: elders, creatures, angels together singing a "new song."[10] Worship, then, can be thought of as a dress rehearsal, preparing us for that future promise when we join the heavenly chorus. Indeed, we are singing with them even now.

"Does Colbert have a choir?" someone recently asked me. Knowing what she meant, I said, "No, although we are planning to assemble a special choir during Lent and Easter this year." However, I really wanted to say, "Yes!" While we may not have a chancel choir, the congregation is the true choir, singing our prayers, participating in a faith that is historical, global, and eschatological, raising our voices in solidarity with the eternal congregation known as the communion of saints, bearing witness to the lordship of Christ, adding to the beauty.

Grace and peace,
Pastor Eric

UTOPIA ELUDED . . . AGAIN

The founders of a new colony, whatever Utopia of human virtue and happiness they might originally project, have invariably recognized it among their earliest practical necessities to allot a portion of the virgin soil as a cemetery, and another portion as the site of a prison.

NATHANIEL HAWTHORNE, *The Scarlet Letter*

If you're like me, you love this country and are grateful to live in it. I love the freedom we have to speak our minds, to worship our gods, and to publish our books. I love our national park system and value our interstate roads. I very much appreciate that we are a government of the people, by the people, and for the people. I am grateful that we have made significant progress in areas such as human rights, animal rights, environmental protection, and health care.

If you're like me, there are also things about our nation that you find deeply disturbing and wish were different. For example, if you compare our country to any of the other twenty advanced democracies in the world comprising the Organisation for Economic Co-operation and Development, you would see that the United States has among the highest rates of child poverty and scores among the lowest on the UN's index of material well-being of children. We have the world's largest prison population and the second-highest rate of water consumption. We are among the top fifteen countries for carbon dioxide output and the top ten countries for homicide.[11] To my way of thinking, these are unacceptable and indefensible realities for the so-called greatest nation on earth.

And if you're like me, despite whatever grievances you may have with the health and direction of our federation, you wouldn't dream of defecting to another country. This is *our* country. We are proud to be passport-carrying United States citizens. It's who we are and it's where we belong, for better and for worse, and many of us are working toward making improvements.

Similarly, many of us have great appreciation and fondness for the Presbyterian church. Significantly, our country and our church had a very similar upbringing, and their respective constitutions were drafted based on many of the same principles. I think it's kind of cool that twelve of the original signers of the Declaration of Independence were Presbyterians,[12] and since that time we have been served by eight Presbyterian presidents.[13] Over the years, Presbyterians have been on the front lines of higher education and medicine, founding colleges and building hospitals. We have been pioneers in mission, with a ministry presence in nearly every country in the world. We don't just preach the gospel; we feed the hungry, we advocate for the oppressed, we mediate peace, and we stand up against systemic injustice.

Of course, we have our share of shortcomings as well. We have made our mistakes, even as we have striven to be faithful and obedient witnesses to the gospel in a broken and complicated world. I acknowledge that there are voices in our church which don't resonate with my own convictions, and there are policies and practices in our denomination with which I disagree, sometimes to the point of moral offense. What's a conscientious person to do?

When Sir Thomas More wrote his book *Utopia* in the sixteenth century, it presumably was a description of a perfect society, and since that time, it has been used as something of a blueprint for people who have experimented with forming ideal communities. But the object of his work was located on a fictitious island somewhere in the Atlantic Ocean. It has never existed outside of some social idealists' minds. Utopia has never, in fact, been achieved.

Utopia, by the way, is based on a compound word from the Greek. *Topos* means place, and the prefix *eu* means good. However, there is another Greek prefix which sounds the same, but with an opposite meaning. *Ou* means no. Whether it's Eutopia or Outopia, the reality may be that the perfectly "good place" is really "no place." Utopia does not and will not exist in either church or society. Pursuing it or insisting on it is an elusive endeavor.

For that reason, I would no sooner leave the Presbyterian church than I would relinquish my citizenship of the United States of America. It's not a perfect church any more than ours is a perfect country. But like other denominations, it belongs to God, and it is sufficient as a vehicle for the Word of God to transform the world. It may not be an ideal place, but it is a good enough place, and an altogether suitable environment for me to honor my vocation. For better and for worse, for the remainder of my baptism, it is *my* place.

Grace and peace,
Pastor Eric

GETTING ALONG

In necessary things unity; in uncertain things freedom; in everything compassion.

ARCHBISHOP MARCO ANTONIA DE DOMINIS,

De Repubblica Ecclesiastica

I HAVE A FRIEND, a computer-tech guy, who describes his work primarily as that of a troubleshooter. "I fix problems; that's my job," he says with a smile. Instead of seeing them as interruptions to his work (the way I often do), he sees problems as his bread and butter. Without problems, he'd be without a paycheck.

The problems we face, in whatever form and field they show up, can be viewed as either nuisances or opportunities. The way we think about them determines how we deal with them. I've been noticing that the problems we face in the church—often rooted, as they are, in controversial issues about which we may not all agree (and not all of them being particularly unique to the church environment)—are variously responded to in one of three "sandy" ways.

Head in the Sand. Sometimes the issues that confront us

are so uncomfortable or fearful that we wish to avoid them altogether, even outright deny their existence. This is the ostrich style of relationships that simply wants the world's difficulties to go away, and by becoming blind, deaf, and dumb to them, we hope to make it so. This strategy works for a short time but only delays the inevitable outcome, thereby exacerbating it.

Line in the Sand. A favorite technique for people who like to flex their muscles, this involves making bold proclamations and taking a firm, confident position. It's Martin Luther, before the Imperial Diet of Worms in 1521, reportedly saying, "My conscience is captive to the Word of God. I cannot and I will not recant anything, for to go against conscience is neither right nor safe. Here I stand. I cannot do otherwise."[14] That line in the sand is what split the church. Draw a line anywhere and it will do that, putting people on either side of an issue, separating people from one another, dividing the body of Christ, as if it's not fractured enough already.

Play in the Sand. This third image—my unabashed favorite—portrays an expansive sandbox in which there is plenty of room for plenty of people, along with plenty of similarities and differences (and, of course, it's those pesky differences that can cause the problems), to play together. It doesn't mean that everyone's doing the same thing or that everyone is best friends with one another. It doesn't even require that everybody there is in ideological, theological, and political alignment with one another, or that there is homogeneity in race, social status, or class. But it does suggest a container that holds a wildly diverse group of people together, reflecting the endless variety contained in the global, historical, catholic body of Christ.

As children of father Abraham, we are heirs to God's promise that his covenant of blessing would be extended to people as numerous as the sands of the world's beaches.[15] Every person who claims Christ as Lord represents one of those grains of sand. And while there is room in the sandbox for everyone, it requires extraordinary love, amazing grace, mutual forbearance, seventy-times-seven forgiveness, holy hospitality, uncommon humility, and endless patience to remain together. That is why many churches have adopted these words as something of a motto:

> In necessary things unity; in uncertain things freedom; in everything compassion.

Many problems are caused when we confuse these categories, assigning essential status to nonessential matters. The one thing necessary is Christ, the one who holds all things (and all people) together. With him as head of the church and Lord of the universe, we don't need to fix all the problems in the world. We just need to practice getting along with one another, until God finally does.

Grace and peace,
Pastor Eric

MAINTAINING FELLOWSHIP

I therefore, the prisoner in the Lord, beg you to lead a life worthy of the calling to which you have been called, with all humility and gentleness, with patience, bearing with one another in love, making every effort to maintain the unity of the Spirit in the bond of peace.

EPHESIANS 4:1-3

IT WAS ONE OF THOSE EXPERIENCES I had as a young pastor which proved to be formative. I was called on to visit a man who was dying, and during the course of the deathbed conversation, I asked him if he would like to say good-bye to anyone. I knew that he had spoken to his daughter because she was the one who summoned me. And I knew from her that she had a brother. When I asked the dying man if he would like to see his son, his angry eyes pierced me, and his words put me back on my heels: "I have *no son*!" Later, I learned that his boy had done something (the details aren't important) which had infuriated him, and the father disowned his son. He went to his grave as though the boy had never existed, and he died a bitter man.

Invariably, at points along the way, either individuals or groups of individuals will do things which provoke us to a kind of righteous indignation which may, for matters of conscience or principle, compel us to break fellowship with them. Sometimes we are motivated out of a sense of justice—distancing ourselves from people or issues with whom we have fundamental disagreements. Other times we are simply acting out our hurt feelings. Sometimes we cut people off in order to protect ourselves from so-called toxic or dangerous people. And sometimes, frankly, we do it because even adults are capable of acting like children.

The biblical way calls us to a different way. When it comes to interpersonal relationships, the ideal is perhaps best captured by the Greek word *homothumadon*, a word the New Testament uses a dozen times to describe the quality of relationships in the early church characterized by an uncommon harmony. They were *together*: a unity of heart, mind, and purpose. Additionally, it is a word which carries a weight that approaches the gravitas of covenant relationships because it reflects the reality that, while disagreements may abound and tensions persist, there is a greater spiritual reality which surpasses the differences, creating unanimity amid diversity of opinion.

Notice I didn't say "uniformity." *Homothumadon* is not the same thing as homogeneity. Biblical unity should not be confused with ecclesiastical cloning. Rather, it's the holy energy which gathers us around the godly value of oneness: one Lord, one faith, one baptism, one God and Father of all.

To be clear, it's less about finding affiliations only with the people who share our particular values, beliefs, and convictions and more about allowing the Holy Spirit to form a single body using many individual and distinct parts. It's a posture that values and honors relationships over ideology, insisting that maintaining God-honoring fellowship is even more important than being right.

I know this is not always possible, and I have personally experienced the reality of broken fellowship in a variety of ways through the years. Sometimes the hurts run too deep, or the disagreements are so severe, or frankly the issues are just so complicated that relationships need to be altered or limited, if not altogether ended. Even the Bible includes accounts of fractured relationships with our heroes of the faith. I have in mind the disagreement Paul and Barnabas had, which "became so sharp that they parted company."[16] Significantly, it was a disagreement which seems to have been resolved at some point later,[17] a reminder that, while breaking fellowship is sometimes a necessary consequence of our human frailty, reconciliation is always the hopeful outcome. Therefore, I earnestly urge you to:

Bear with one another in love.

Practice mutual forbearance.

Make every effort to maintain the unity of the Spirit in the bond of peace.

I *beg* this of you.

Grace and peace,
Pastor Eric

BIBLIOPHILE

In the beginning was the Word . . .
JOHN 1:1

I COULD JUST TELL YOU that I am fond of words, but I'd rather say that I'm a lexiconophalist. For a number of reasons, I like words. I like the sound of them, both in this and other languages. I love to speak certain words in particular, simply for the way they roll off the tongue. *Flabbergasted* is one of my favorite words to say out loud. But it's in good company with a handful of others: *Zamboni*, *tomfoolery*, *bamboozle*, and *sassafras* among them. My most recent favorite, although I have infrequent occasion to use it, is *sesquipedalian*. (It means to be characterized by the use of long words.) And who among us doesn't like to say *Beelzebub*? (Go ahead; say it out loud.) I'm sure it would show up in the baby-names books if it wasn't one of the proper names for the devil.

I am intrigued by the complex phenomenon that putting certain words together and constructing sentences results in our ability to communicate ideas with one another. I marvel at the way language keeps evolving as we find new ways to communicate. "Truthiness," for example, coined by comedian Steven Colbert, made its way into the dictionary in 2006, and was granted the coveted "new word of the year" designation.[18] By the way, it refers to truth that is derived from the gut rather than from books, making it a quintessential postmodern word.

Words are pretty important, both for good and for bad—a fact that didn't go unnoticed by God. Words can bless, and words can curse. When God began to bustle about the work of creating somethingness out of nothingness, the medium was words. I think that must be why the Hebrew word *dabar* means both word and deed. God says a word and it makes something happen: *light*, *sky*, *earth*, *seas*, *humankind*. Those were among the first words (here in translation) uttered by God, according to the biblical witness. The words turned into stuff. Good stuff.

Which, I also happen to believe, is why Jesus was identified as the Word-Made-Flesh.[19] Back in the beginning, when those first creative words were uttered, they originated from none other than the *logos*—the Word. "All things came into being through him," the Scripture insists.[20] Whether in Hebrew or in Greek, Jesus is both *dabar* and *logos*: God's perfect Word which became God's perfect Action. God gave great dignity to humanity by becoming a human.

Simultaneously, God gave dignity to words by coming not only *with* words but as *the* Word, who was, of course, both a noun and a verb.

All of which is a terribly wordy, albeit fun way of getting to the point of this missive: the church library.

As books contain words and libraries contain books, they are containers for lots of words. And most libraries are—like the human body (think blood)—closed systems of circulation. Books are typically catalogued, checked out, read, returned, and reshelved.

But a distinctively *missional* congregational culture looks different from what is typical. Here, everyone and everything is *sent* by our sending God. Our library, therefore, is not intended to be a repository or a collection or a place to keep and preserve books. It is, rather, as our whole church is meant to be, a place of assembling for the purpose of distributing. People come together here and are then gently thrust into the world. Books are gathered and are then shared and used.

So here's the deal: Our church has a *missional* library. Books (as well as tapes, videos, and compact discs) come and go, and (with the hoped-for exception of the reference material) sometimes they don't come back. I hope you'll browse the shelves of books, take one home, read it well. And if it makes you think of someone who might benefit by reading it, pass it along; it will do more good in the hands of a friend than on the shelves of our library. There's no check-out procedure. Just take a book that looks good. Keep it, or return it, or pass it on. Conversely, if you've read a book that you think others should read, donate it to the library. Just be warned: You may not see it again.

Grace and peace,
Pastor Eric

PARENTAL DISCRETION ADVISED

Q: When is the right time for my child to start taking Communion?

BACK IN THE DAY, children were routinely baptized as infants and raised in "the nurture and admonition of the Lord."[21] At some point during adolescence, they "confirmed" their baptism by publicly professing their faith, after which time they were welcomed as full communicants to the Lord's Table.

The elders at Colbert—recognizing that faith development does not follow a prescribed pattern or time line, and not wanting to either unduly hasten or delay the time at which a person participates in Holy Communion—has decided that parents are in the best position to determine when their children are ready to receive the sacrament. The Bible gives only indirect guidance in this matter.

What we see in Jesus is a special (and countercultural) affinity for children: welcoming them, blessing them, and issuing strong warnings against any who would cause one of them to stumble ("better for you if a great millstone were hung around your neck and you were thrown into the sea").[22] Following his lead, we strive at Colbert to create a safe, welcoming environment for everyone, but especially children, "for it is to such as these that the kingdom of God belongs."[23]

Just as children have a place around our home dinner tables even though they cannot always enter fully into adult conversation, our children are welcome at the Lord's Table. In their early years, parents present children for a special blessing, but at some point it is appropriate for them to receive the elements, even if they don't fully understand what it all means (but then again, who among us fully grasps this mystery?). Just when that time is will vary from person to person.

One couple I admire decided that when their children were able to articulate their faith to another person who was not a family member, they were ready to partake of the sacrament. I like that. However you make the decision, my hope is that it involves a conversation with your child (and preferably not in the moments immediately leading up to Communion!) helping them to understand that this is not a snack break in worship but that it is a holy occasion when we remember God's sacrificial love for us in the giving of his Son.

Like so many things, the church has, over time, added layers of rules and restrictions to control how Communion is to be celebrated. But while there have been good reasons for such regulation, it has, in my considered opinion, created the unintended consequence of making God seem even more aloof, distant, and inaccessible to us.

While I like to think that I have a high view of the sacraments, that's not the same thing as making them hard to access. The invitation to "come to the table" is Jesus saying, "Come to me." And that may be the very definition of an open, expansive, and inclusive call to discipleship, one that is within everyone's reach. Because if there's one thing that Jesus is afraid of, it's that someone gets left out.

Grace and peace,
Pastor Eric

PS—There are few pastoral conversations I enjoy more than those related to the sacraments. If you need a little help talking to your children about this, invite me to your house.

THE BYSTANDER EFFECT

Now by chance a priest was going down that road; and when he saw him, he passed by on the other side.

LUKE 10:31

I FIRST READ ABOUT IT some years ago in the magazine *Orion*—the one must-subscribe-to periodical that my parents give me every year as a birthday gift. It's called "the bystander effect," referring to the phenomenon in which the greater the number of people there are present in a situation, the less likely people are to respond to a need or a crisis.[24] When an emergency situation occurs, observers are more likely to take action if there are few or no other witnesses. For example, if you encountered a wounded person on the sidewalk in downtown Spokane, you would be much more likely to stop and help if nobody else was around than if you were being shuffled along in a crowd.

After years of research, social scientists have identified two major factors which contribute to the bystander effect.[25] First, *the presence of other people creates a diffusion of responsibility.*

Because there are other observers, individuals do not feel as much pressure to take action, since the responsibility to take action is thought to be shared among all of those present.

The second reason is *the need to behave in correct and socially acceptable ways.* When other observers in a group fail to react, individuals often take this as a signal that a response is not needed or not appropriate. It's peer pressure in its passive form. Especially when the need appears to be ambiguous in nature, we are reluctant to get involved for fear of making a mistake (and doing more harm than good) or for fear of making a fool of ourselves because we misjudged the situation.

This, it seems to me, is both a sociological and an ecclesiastical phenomenon. That is to say, people in the church may not be any more likely to come to the assistance of a person in need than anybody else in society. You need look no further than the parable Jesus told about the Good Samaritan. The religious leaders identified in the story failed to make a loving response toward a neighbor in need, while an ordinary man on the street, though presumably disdained by the injured man, took care of him. Compassion, the text suggests, compelled him to act.

The even more interesting thing is that once you are made aware of the bystander effect, it loses its power, providing a kind of psychological immunity against it. Perhaps the Good Samaritan understood this and knew that a parade of priests, Levites, and other so-called religious people would succumb to the bystander effect and walk by on the other side of the road while a person in need was ignored. The Samaritan took responsibility and offered assistance and care (up to a point), defying the tendency to assume that some other, more available, more qualified person would step in.

The gravitational force of a missional church like ours is to move toward people in need. We don't assume that another church or another individual or the New Hope Resource Center or one of many government agencies is going to take care of them. We ourselves take responsibility (again, not always *full* responsibility) for the people we encounter who are in need of some kindness. Even more, missionally minded congregations don't wait for such people to approach us; rather, we seek them out and look for creative and sustainable ways to love our neighbors as ourselves.

With this bit of information, consider yourselves inoculated from the bystander effect.

Grace and peace,
Pastor Eric

DON'T SWEAT THE ADIAPHORA

. . . making every effort to maintain the unity of the Spirit in the bond of peace.

EPHESIANS 4:3

IT IS INCREASINGLY and disturbingly the case that as the church interacts with and speaks into the broader world, it is becoming known and identified more by what it's against than what it's for. The church has joined the academy in being addicted to dispute, critique, and negation when it should privilege wisdom and wonder.

Taking a stand and standing firm, come hell or high water and irrespective of the damage done to relationships, is seen as virtuous, commendable, courageous. But when it results in injury to people, it necessarily brings those stances into question. When following the Jesus way, it's pretty hard to justify collateral damage for the sake of the Kingdom of God, particularly when the damage hurts the children of God.

Balancing truth and grace is seldom easy. The task of maintaining the unity of the church is enormously complicated because Christianity was birthed in controversy. Blame it on its founder and head if you wish; Jesus did much to disrupt the social and political norms of his day, including changing the definition of mother, brother, and sister (those who do the will of God).[26] He didn't just color outside the lines, he completely rearranged them, breaking sabbath rules, for example, through the audacious claim that he was its Lord. After his resurrection, this led to all sorts of questions about how the gospel way of life was to be lived, especially as it involved implications for people groups like men and women, Jews and Gentiles, slaves and free. But the questions extended into a variety of ethical areas as the grace of Christ collided with the law of Moses. One of the early controversies that threatened the fellowship in Corinth was over the question of whether a Christian could eat food that had been sacrificed to an idol. Here's how Saint Paul mediated the topic:

> Food does not bring us near to God; we are no worse if we do not eat, and no better if we do.
>
> Be careful, however, that the exercise of your rights does not become a stumbling block to the weak.
>
> 1 CORINTHIANS 8:8-9, NIV

Do you see what he did there? He did not answer the question in a yes-or-no way. He lifted it out of its binary quagmire and redirected their concern from a matter of food to a matter of fellowship—something much more precious.

Relationships trump rules. As Leonard Sweet, my friend and teacher, is fond of saying, "You can either be right, or you can be in a relationship."

Over the years we have gradually and variously expanded these binaries to such categories as black and white, gay and straight, Catholic and Protestant, dunking or sprinkling, physical or spiritual presence, to create categories of inclusion and exclusion, right and wrong, orthodoxy and heresy.

At some point in the midst of a sea of controversies and disagreements, the church adopted the notion of adiaphora—matters over which good, faithful, God-fearing Christians can disagree and still get along—and also remain in God's good grace. For example, on which day of the week we are to observe the sabbath. Or the place and importance of praying in tongues. These are among the many nonessential matters of faith. The holy Scriptures insist that in Christ, the binaries dissolve into a strange, mishmash unity known as the church. There is, and intentionally so, very little about it that is homogeneous.

But those dratted differences are what threaten the peace and unity of the church, thus the need for a refresher in adiaphora. It's high time we reclaim the concept, loosening our grip (or letting go entirely) of the issues that are conflicting and inflicting the body of Christ for the sake of maintaining the unity of the Spirit, getting along with one another amid our considerable disagreements. There are a lot of people we don't like and with whom we disagree that we are going to spend eternity with because Jesus died for us all, so we'd better start practicing getting along now. If it's not on the key ring of the Kingdom of God, it's probably not worth sweating over. Getting along with people is more important than defending one's principles.

After all, Jesus went about breaking a lot of rules in order to fulfill the law of love.

Grace and peace,
Pastor Eric

THE COMPANY OF WINNOWERS

His winnowing fork is in his hand . . .
LUKE 3:17

ONE SATURDAY NIGHT some weeks ago, I stopped by the church to grab a book I had left behind in my study. The building was dark and quiet, and I wasn't in a hurry, so I took a detour into the sanctuary for no particular reason other than that I'm fond of it as a holy meeting place. After meandering around a bit, I ended up in the pulpit, awash in moonlight coming through the clerestory windows, and caressed the seductive slab of ponderosa pine which retains the live edges of the massive tree from which it was milled on the Olympic Peninsula.

Admittedly, this next part is a little weird: Addressing the pulpit, I was surprised to hear myself say out loud, "I love you. And I hate you." Fortunately, it didn't talk back to me, but the intervening silence that followed was like one of those surprise gifts that sometimes show up in dark, quiet, unscheduled, and unpopulated places. As strange as it was for me for the first time to speak *to*, rather than *from* that pulpit, it revealed the love-hate relationship I have with preaching.

- I love the discipline of being immersed in the holy Scriptures—those inspired and authoritative words of God. I consider the Bible to be an inexhaustible mine of holy treasures.
- I enjoy the intellectual-spiritual interplay of studying, researching, thinking, brooding, reading, stewing, pondering, praying, questioning, wrestling, wondering, surrendering.
- I appreciate (perhaps *honor* is the better word) the creative, messy, mysterious process of crafting a sermon.
- I delight in new insights, ahas, and the occasional epiphany when I feel like I'm being tutored one-on-one by the Holy Spirit. Frequently the thought occurs to me that "someone must be praying for me."
- I feel humbled that, with varying degrees of clarity and consistency, I get to be a mouthpiece for God's Word.
- I am grateful for the ways that preparing sermons has a transformative effect on me personally.

Frequently, as I am walking across the parking lot to my car on Sunday afternoons, accompanied by that wonderful feeling of being utterly spent, yet deeply satisfied, I pray it out loud—a question that has worked its way into the liturgy of my life: "Why do I get to do this?" My ordination to a ministry of Word and sacrament feels like such a gift, a holy privilege: helping to keep this community God-attentive. It's a big piece, I believe, of what I was made for.

So it's mostly a love relationship, I suppose, but there are some things about preaching that I don't like, or at least parts of it that I struggle against. Mostly, I don't like the isolation—the largely solitary experience that leads up to Sunday morning. Besides, it strikes me as unlikely, at the least, maybe even a little arrogant, that one person would be able to fully and accurately hear God's Word all by him- or herself.

Being a communitarian both by theology and by disposition, I'd like to try an experiment this year, a twist on something we've done before. Over the years, we have gathered at various times and during special seasons for the old, corporate style of Bible study known as *lectio divina* (literally "sacred reading"). My experience as a participant in *lectio* gatherings, over the span of two decades, is that I always, without fail, hear or see something in the text that I had missed on my own. *Lectio divina* has taught me the wisdom of corporate Bible study where the richness of ideas and insights of others illuminates the passage beyond my own ability.

Introducing "The Company of Winnowers."

Winnowing is an agrarian word describing the ancient (and in some developing countries, the still-modern) act of separating grain from chaff. Whether it's wheat or rice or some other grain, the part that we consume must first be separated from husks and stalks. The oldest method for doing this involves stabbing a pile of freshly harvested grain with a pitchfork and tossing it up into the open air, thereby allowing the lighter, worthless chaff to get blown away by the wind, while the heavier, edible pieces fall to the floor.

Because of its powerful imagery, winnowing has taken on additional, figurative meanings as well, to refer to any process of sorting out or discerning what is most valuable or helpful and leaving the rest behind. Which brings me, at long last, to the point.

I am extending an open invitation for any of you to join me in this work this year, by gathering around the next Sunday's text each Tuesday afternoon at 3:30. We will take a stab at the text, toss it up to the winds of the Spirit, and see what is left after some of it gets blown away. We will ask, seek, and knock.[27] We will pray, and we will listen. We will share insights, and ask questions, and perhaps even argue from time to time. But however we go about it, we will be trying to answer this fundamental question: "What is the Word of God, through this text, trying to say to this congregation this week?" And we will do it by allowing the Holy Spirit, winnowing its way through this community, to reveal the divine presence, awakening us to a new *way*, to grace-tempered-*truth*, to abundant *life*.

I would be very glad for your company.

Grace and peace,
Pastor Eric

WOOD AND NAILS

O Christ, the Master Carpenter,
who at the last, through wood and nails,
purchased our whole salvation,
wield well your tools in the workshop of your world,
so that we who come rough-hewn to your bench
may here be fashioned to a truer beauty by your hand.

IONA ABBEY WORSHIP BOOK

When it comes to making and repairing, God's preferred means are words. Out of nothing at all, God's spoken word creates brand-new people and things ("Let there be light!"), and then God's spoken word redeems the people and things which have been deranged by sin and death ("Lazarus, come out!").[28] Whenever God speaks, something significant is bound to happen.

However, in the economy of the Kingdom, words are not the only means available to fix people and things gone bad. God has also seen fit to use material objects as agents of re-creation. When God's word—in a magnificent display of self-revelation—"became flesh and blood, and moved into the neighborhood," it took on physical characteristics which happen to look very much like you and me.[29] The coupling of word and sacrament is epitomized in the life of Christ, who took on not only the fullness of our humanity but also the entirety of our physical life, including the stuff of our existence. Consider this:

- When Jesus first entered the world, the container for the Christ child was a Bethlehem feed trough. His welcome mat to this world was a manger made of wood and nails.
- As he grew up, Jesus took it from there. Raised as the son of a carpenter, becoming familiar with the tools of that noble trade, becoming fond of the smell of fresh-cut wood, he became skillful with hammer and nails. At the age of thirty-three, when he purchased our salvation on a Calvary cross, his adult body was—as his infant body once was—again, in intimate contact with wood and nails.

In other words, wood and nails are the stuff of *incarnation* and *crucifixion*. They were among the holy materials present and necessary on the occasions of Christ's birth and death. But that's not all. Since the body of Christ continues to live on as the church, there's more.

About fifteen hundred years later, when the church was careening off the twin rails of truth and grace, a young Augustinian monk launched an ecclesiastical revolution when he nailed his now-famous ninety-five theses to the wooden door of a church in Wittenberg, Germany. Wood and nails, you see, are also the stuff of *reformation*.

As I survey the buildings that have been constructed on our church site over the last two decades, I am mindful of the many board feet of wood and the many cases of nails that were used in creating this outpost for the mission of God in North Spokane County. And while our buildings and grounds are beautiful, there are flaws in the actual ministry that we have undertaken together. The imperfections which riddle our work (this will be obvious to anybody) cannot be fixed through wood and nails, but they can, nonetheless, be remedied through the kind of personal humility that is receptive to repentance and open to change.

Our reformation door, with its wood and nails at the ready, is a standing testimony to these changes that are courting our attention: issues, ideas, and behaviors that need to be subjected to the hand of our Master Carpenter, so that—by embracing incarnation, crucifixion, and reformation—we can be fashioned to a truer beauty.

Grace and peace,
Pastor Eric

ADAPTIVE CHALLENGES

The annoying thing about plans is how rare it is for everything to go just right.
LAURENCE GONZALES, *Deep Survival*

MURPHY'S LAW, the adage that "whatever can go wrong will," has caused many people to label Murphy a pessimist, but he was right. It's not that something will always go wrong in every single situation, but that in every sort of circumstance, and in everyone's life, something eventually will go wrong. It's simply a part of living in a world fraught with complexities and chaos and sin. There are no fail-safe immunities against problems, no promises to insure pain avoidance, no guarantees that our dreams will be fully realized. Despite the best plans, the best training, and the best resources, sooner or later something will get off course or flat-out fail, presenting us with an adaptive challenge: Can we make the necessary adjustments and modify our goals in light of current issues?

When my sixteen-year-old and I went into Mount Rainier National Park last month, we did so with the intention of hiking the ninety-three-mile trail around the mountain. But after only fifteen miles into the backcountry, we encountered bad weather and even worse blisters, and we made the decision to come off the trail. When Sadie later asked me if I was disappointed, I said, "Honey, I've hiked the Wonderland Trail before. My goal was to spend this time with you, and I don't really care how or where we do that; I'm just happy to be with you."

There is an old saying that there are no old, bold mountain climbers. The old ones learned to respect the conditions which sometimes meant they didn't reach the summit; the bold ones are dead. If we become so goal-oriented that we become blind to the warning signals along the way, we may be heading for disaster. While perseverance and long-suffering are typically virtuous, rigidity and stubbornness can be lethal for individuals, for relationships, and for organizations.

The biblical witness offers ample evidence of God's immutable nature (the same yesterday, today, and forever)[30]—and that he is flexible, finding ever-creative ways to meet us. It's what someone once described to me as being "solid in the center, but soft around the edges." In a rapidly changing world, God's character does not mutate one little bit; it is altogether steadfast and consistent. But the *ways* that God is actively bringing about the miracles of salvation and liberation, in our lives and in our world, are new every morning. When it comes to reconciling relationships, God has a limitless capacity for adaptation, and goes to extreme, sacrificial measures to love us and to heal us.

We are at no loss for adaptive challenges to test us. Let us hold firm to that solid core of our baptismal identity—the most enduring and consequential of relationships—while remaining soft and flexible around the edges so that we can best honor and protect the sacred nature of our relationships with one another.

Grace and peace,
Pastor Eric

DOES THE FUTURE HAVE A CHURCH?

Political [or denominational] *loyalties can never be as deep or as broad as the bond that unites believers in Christ.*
MARK NOLL, *The American Revolution*

The Presbyterian Church (U.S.A.) is facing mighty challenges these days, even as our own young congregation is thriving. The disturbing, declining trends stand in juxtaposition to our own growth and vibrancy. For example, did you know that denominationally, we lose about 180,000 members a year, and between 2004 and 2005, we had a net loss of fifty-nine congregations? Because of a steady, forty-five-year decline, the Presbyterian Church is now just about half the size it was the year I was born.

There are a number of reasons for these trends, and in fact, most denominations are singing some arrangement of the "Mainline Blues" these days. We are seeing more congregations close their doors because they have become too small to sustain their ministry, and we're seeing more churches protest denominational decisions by cutting off their financial support or by making plans to altogether sever their ties to the larger body. Additionally, numerous "renewal organizations" are attempting to reform the mission and systems of the church. In short, denominational health, relevance, and loyalty are at an all-time low.

As you are probably aware, one of the interdenominational hot potato issues that we're dealing with across the country involves discussion and dissension around the place of homosexual persons in the church, particularly in positions of leadership. Typically, it is this issue which gets cited or blamed as churches consider whether to stick with their respective denominations. It's consuming an enormous, inordinate even, amount of energy and has become something of a line in the sand that threatens to divide the church.

From my perspective, if we're talking about making relationship-ending decisions based on biblical morality, I can think of a lot of other deal-breaking issues besides sexual orientation that would top the list. There is, it seems to me, a disproportionate amount of energy preoccupying the church these days around issues of sexuality while all around us, people are, quite literally, dying. These are days that have some people anxiously asking, "Does the church have a future?" Personally, I think that's the wrong question. The more important question is, "Does the future have a church?"

The analogy that comes to mind is the relationship between a church's building and that church's ministry. One way to think about a church building is like a museum: It is there to hold and preserve great traditions, art, truth, and memories. They are containers of archives, artifacts, and various records. In this scenario, people relate to the buildings by honoring, respecting, and taking care of them. As buildings age, a great deal of time and money can be spent maintaining and restoring them.

Another way to understand a church building is as an outpost for mission. Its purpose is to provide facilities for doing the work of God. The physical space of a church is merely an instrument for worship, education, fellowship, evangelism, and discipleship to help people assume and live out their baptismal identity—a distinctively missional, or "sent out" identity. The purpose is to serve people and glorify God, not to become servants to structures.

At Colbert, we tend to lean more toward the "mission outpost" rather than the "museum" end of the continuum. As a stewardship issue, it's certainly important for us to *care* for our facilities, but it's even more important for us to *use* them to fulfill our mission. I don't expect this to happen in my lifetime, but at the point at which the buildings no longer serve the mission, they should either be sold or razed.

Denominations have the same function: They are institutional containers, providing structures and systems to assist congregations in doing mission. And when they no longer serve that function, they need to either adapt or disappear. There is nothing inherently valuable about either a building or a denomination when its form fails to serve its function.

It always makes me uneasy when I hear people say, "I love

the Presbyterian Church," a sentiment which strikes me as edging dangerously close to idolatry. Anytime a structure, whether it's a building or an organization, displaces our primary allegiance to Christ, we run the risk of living vicariously through another entity and depersonalizing our faith in Jesus.

Personally, and for what it's worth, I can't even muster a modicum of anxiety about the future of the church because I know the church has a future, one which is held firmly in God's hands. My guess is that the Presbyterian Church (U.S.A.) is going to look significantly different a generation from now, if it exists at all, because sometimes denominations need to be remodeled, other times they need to be demolished. But whatever happens, whatever institutional evolution or deconstruction that takes place in the years ahead, I am confident that there will be a way for us to maintain faith in our Lord and sustain faithfulness to the mission to which he has called us.

That the Presbyterian Church, as we now know it, has a future is highly questionable. That the future has a church, inasmuch as it is God's primary vessel for exhibiting the Kingdom of God, is indisputable. There are plenty of things worth losing sleep over. The church of the future isn't one of them.

Grace and peace,
Pastor Eric

COMPENSATION PACKAGE

Bear one another's burdens, and in this way
you will fulfill the law of Christ.
GALATIANS 6:2

"I LOVE THAT SONG, but I don't agree with some of the words. And when we get to one particular line, I don't sing them." It was a comment made to me by a friend within our worshipping community, and something about it touched me and impressed me on a couple of levels. First, I found myself feeling appreciative of his maturity. His comment was accompanied by a spirit of humility, without even a trace of defiance or criticism. He wouldn't think of boycotting worship, leaving the church, or complaining to the session about our choice of music. Rather, he recognizes that he can be a part of both a congregation and a larger communion of saints and sinners with whom he doesn't always agree. Theological and ideological uni*formity* is not the same thing as (and is not a prerequisite for) *comm*unity. The body of Christ can be diverse without being divisive.

Secondly, it was a reminder to me that we are able to compensate for one another during times of doubt, weakness, and struggle. While I happen to agree with my friend's theological grievance about some of the words in that particular song, it was good to know that such agreement is not a prerequisite for whether or not the church keeps singing its songs.

I think this is one of the brilliant and beautiful aspects of the body of Christ: There is a sense of unity and wholeness amid the individual parts. And at any given time, some of those parts may be ill or hurting or doubting or ensnared in sin. But the overall health and strength of the body can compensate during times of individual weakness.

I remember once meeting with a young man who was absolutely engulfed in the god-awful darkness of a deep depression. He saw no way out of it, and he could see no purpose to living. He was clearly suicidal, having both a plan and the lethal means to carry it out. I had to admit that his life was, in fact, overwhelmingly grim, a pile of circumstances that would make just about anybody say, "If this is life, what's the point in living?" And even though I couldn't see the exit door to his personal hell, I remained hopeful that God could deliver him.

I asked him to do me one personal favor. Although noncommittal, he was willing to listen. I said, "I want you to borrow my faith. I believe that God loves you and has hopes for you. And I believe that God is bigger than this, and that you can outlive this pain. Will you give God a chance? For just one week, promise me that you will stay alive." At a moment when he wasn't even sure that God existed, based on the strength of our friendship, he was willing and able to borrow my faith—just long enough for God to lift him out of the pit of despair. Now, years later, that man is alive. And quite well.

I have been on the receiving end of this compensation of grace through my involvement in this beloved community as well. There was a season in my life, not so long ago, in which I was unable to recite the Lord's Prayer in its entirety; every Sunday for nearly a year as I was leading you in worship, I would choke on the words "as we forgive those who have sinned against us." I simply could not say them. And as much as it troubled me and signaled to me that I still had some hard, holy work ahead of me, I also took great comfort that you all were praying those words for me. Not only was the prayer itself not dependent on my solo voice to reach the divine ears but I found myself being carried on the power of your prayers. It was truly a sweet moment for me when I once again rejoined you in praying those words accompanied, as they were, with new and profound meaning.

This is a foundational aspect of our life together: In the alternating seasons of our lives, we find ourselves on the giving and the receiving ends of the grace of God which compensates and carries, borrowing other's faith, bearing one another's burdens, fulfilling the law of Christ.

Grace and peace,
Pastor Eric

WRITING THE FIFTH GOSPEL

How beautiful upon the mountains
are the feet of the messenger who announces peace,
who brings good news,
who announces salvation,
who says to Zion, "Your God reigns."
ISAIAH 52:7

The story of the Good News of Jesus Christ was first written down by Matthew, Mark, Luke, and John and then handed down to each subsequent generation. But why not just one, coherent account, instead of the four we've been given? Some argue that each of them brings a unique perspective on Jesus, emphasizing different aspects of his life and ministry that, together, give us a fuller, more accurate view. While I agree with that position, I would also suggest that another reason might be to show us how four different people understood, described, and lived the Good News. That is to say, it demonstrates that—while there is considerable common ground—there is not a one-size-fits-all style of discipleship. We each *wear* Christ a bit differently from one another.

Over the years, some people have found the apparent

contradictions or inconsistencies in the four accounts troubling, calling into question things like the authority, the inspiration, and the inerrancy of these supposedly sacred texts. After all, if it truly is the Word of God, you'd think (so goes the argument) that it would be clear and concise. But if you understand the stories as somewhat subjective reflections, personalized for the ways each of the four authors understood and experienced the message of salvation, it suggests that, in the ever-creative ways of God, the story gets customized uniquely within each individual who receives it. In other words, the way to integrate these four somewhat distinct texts is by internalizing them, indeed to *live* them. When the gospel is thus lived, the ones through whom it is living become the holy agents of evangelism, simultaneously following in the footsteps of apostolic authority and celebrating the particularities of each new, Good News context of its telling.

Which leads to the proposal for a congregational experiment. During the weeks of Lent this year, the art corner of our sanctuary will be designated as a place to display—in words and images—the ways you are observing and experiencing how Jesus is among us, how Jesus is for us. Like the original four Gospels, it may include your questions, your doubts, and your failures, as well as your expressions of faith and praise. It may describe God's presence, and it may wonder about God's silence. Indeed, if the cross is instructive, it may at times read much more like bad news rather than good. Whatever it includes, it will be our corporate attempt to bear witness to the Paschal Mystery (Christ has died, Christ is risen, Christ will come again) while testifying to the reality of the reign of Christ as it continues to steadily emerge, even as it is being variously received and resisted.

Yes, the canon of holy Scripture was officially closed some sixteen hundred years ago. But the Story isn't yet finished. It is being told and lived and re-storied through the likes of people who yet incarnate—in loving deeds and truth-filled words—the presence of Jesus resurrected, alive, and well, reigning and residing among us.

So take up a pen, and take up your life, and write the next verse. And make it good.

Grace and peace,
Pastor Eric

4

—

What Following Jesus Is About

ONCE UPON A TIME

In him you also . . . were marked with the seal of the promised Holy Spirit . . .
EPHESIANS 1:13

I GREW UP IN A FAMILY that told stories. Some were true and some were fictitious. The fiction—which was my favorite genre—usually included a Norwegian troll or two, some magic, and a near-death experience of some kind. From those stories, I learned that the world was full of danger lurking about and life was never safe. My grandmother, the Reverend Evelyn Hoiland Peterson, was the master storyteller in our family. But she didn't just tell the stories; she embodied them. She *became* the characters. And she must have been a good actress because I remember being regularly terrified by her.

My kids, fortunately, have grandparents that they grew up cuddling with as stories were being told or read. My grandmother, on the other hand, was a force to be reckoned with. She intimidated me. There were times, in fact, when she, quite frankly, scared me. I credit her for instilling within me a healthy "fear of the Lord."

The late Evelyn Peterson was a good woman. She was a Pentecostal pastor who organized a new church in Bigfork, Montana, and a godlier woman you're not likely to ever meet. But she had fire in her veins and a fierceness that defied femininity. The stories she told were a strange mixture of fiction and nonfiction, almost never, I now believe, exclusively one or the other. Looking back on them, I realize that such distinctions didn't matter; she was teaching me about the world, and from her I learned a great deal about the shaping forces of good and evil, fear and love, failure and victory, God and the devil. She was a good storyteller.

But she wasn't the only one, and sometimes the entirely true stories outrivaled the highly imaginative and embellished ones. There are some things that some people do that are so bizarre you just can't fabricate them. And chances are, if you've lived in Montana for any length of time, you already have a clue as to what I'm talking about. As my whole extended family on the Peterson side of the genealogical tree gathered every year for a Big Sky vacation, we spent a good deal of time exchanging stories while roasting marshmallows.

Sitting around a bonfire one night on the shore of Flathead Lake (I believe it was the summer of 1976), my uncle Miles, an Assemblies of God pastor in Polson, told a story that has stuck with me ever since. It happened once upon a late spring morning when, after a typical two-and-a-half-hour charismatic worship service complete with speaking in tongues, the entire congregation reassembled themselves down on the banks of the Flathead River, just below the outlet of the lake.

Her name was Angela, a woman in her early thirties who had recently made a decision to follow Christ. She was a very large person, and she slowly waded out waist-deep in the cold water to join my uncle, who stood waiting for her in his sacramental hip waders. Uncle Miles prayed with her, and then, as he had done a hundred times before, leaned her back to fully immerse her in the water. The one thing Angela apparently didn't tell him, or perhaps hoped would be transformed by her new life in Christ, was a fear of water. And when the cold waters of the Flathead River swallowed her up, she panicked. Grabbing onto the only semisolid handhold available, she did a vise grip on my uncle's arms, pulling him under the water with her.

The story at this point is best told by my cousins, who were sitting with the rest of the congregation on the shore, singing old gospel hymns. According to Kevin and Kim—who, by the way, later defected from the Assemblies and became Presbyterian pastors—there was a furious moment or two of white water thrashing and a tangle of arms and legs and hip waders until finally, due to either adrenaline or the Holy Spirit or a combination of the two, depending on who you ask, Miles mustered the strength to break free from the woman's panicked death grip and came up for air. Afterward, he cautiously assisted the new child of God back on her feet and escorted her to dry land, where they joined the rest of the body of Christ for a picnic lunch of fried chicken, potato salad, and deviled eggs.

I hadn't thought about that story for years until this last week. At the time, in the summer of '76, it was told amid a great deal of falling-off-your-stump laughter, earning big points in the family contest of the storytelling hall of fame. But I wonder now if that story hasn't had an unwitting effect on my understanding of the wonder and the surprise and the danger associated with baptism.

Baptism is the beginning point and ending point of life. It's where we are grafted into Christ as infant or adult, and it's the place from which we are ushered into eternity. It is crucifixion and resurrection. It's a beginning and an end. And there is so much that falls in between. But in it all and through it all and even despite it all, it's the clear and defining moment in each of our lives when we receive God's hearty and irrevocable endorsement. I am fully persuaded of this: There is nothing else able to make joy—God's and ours—so complete.

Grace and peace,
Pastor Eric

IDENTITY CRISIS

Who am I? They mock me, these lonely questions of mine.
Whoever I am, Thou knowest, O God, I am thine!
DIETRICH BONHOEFFER, "Who Am I?"

North Americans suffer from a crisis of identity. I'm not sure this is necessarily something new, but it seems to me that, with an increasingly large and diverse menu of options from which to choose and a crescendo of voices vying for not only our attention but our allegiance, it's a tricky thing to figure out our personal ID. Where are the voices that can be trusted to accurately tell us the truth about ourselves? Few things are so consequential as this, for when we don't know who we really are, we find it impossible to really live. Our lifestyles, in other words, originate from and emerge out of our understanding of ourselves. There may be no more important question for us to both ask and answer than the one Bonhoeffer posed in a 1945 poem he wrote from a Nazi prison cell within months of his execution: *Who am I?*

Depending on what we consider to be important, or

who's asking the question of us, we might define ourselves (and, by extension, what we value) by such things as:

- Religious affiliation
- Political party
- Dietary preferences
- Personality types
- Gender
- Family of origin
- Vocation
- Special-interest groups, clubs, and hobbies
- Education
- Income tax bracket
- Relational status
- Ethnicity
- Physical and mental health

A culture like ours, which spends enormous amounts of money and energy trying to convince us that our value as people is inextricably related to our ability to consume and to produce—and in both cases, the more the better—you can see why I often feel like I'm up against some formidable competition, to the point where—if the "game" is directing the desires of peoples' hearts—I frequently feel like I'm on the losing team.

I have become convinced that, with so much at stake (nothing less than our very souls), nothing shy of a sacramental response is what is needed. Spend much time around the

Presbyterian church in Colbert, and you're going to notice this emphasis. So much, in fact, that it led someone recently to ask about it. I think I recall accurately the exact quote: "Dude, what is your *thing* with baptism? You talk about it so much; what gives? I don't get it!"

Although I'm in the process of writing a doctoral dissertation that hopefully answers that question, my interest is far more than an academic exercise; rather, it emerges out of a deep pastoral concern. My primary vocational responsibility is related to my commitment to be a follower of the Way of Jesus—namely, to help you live into your identity as children of God. But what has the staying power? What remains relevant and endurable? The answer is both tried and true, while not the least bit tired.

In the storied waters of baptism, we are given a new identity, assigned a new purpose, animated with a new life. God is making all things new, and we are participants and players in the redemptive acts of the ever-new creation. Like nothing else, baptism captures (and then captivates) us with the mighty acts of God, who brings order out of chaos, washes away sin, delivers people from bondage into freedom, ransoms our lives with the life of his own Son, and fills us with the Holy Spirit so that our lives can spill—cornucopia-like—with the holy virtues of love, joy, peace, patience, kindness, generosity, faithfulness, gentleness, and self-control. "You will know [read: *identify*] them by their fruits."[1]

More important than anything—and this, I believe, will be among the chief criteria for whether or not I am judged to be a pastoral success—is whether you know, in the very deepest parts of your being, that you belong to Christ, and that you have been claimed with the everlasting grace of God. Far above the cacophony and confusion of all the other voices that are trying to ID you, my greatest desire is that you are able to hear the voice of the one who desires to be ever more intimately the Lover of your soul, the one who can't help but smile at the mere thought of you, the one who takes endless pleasure in you, the one who—with the unmatched fierceness of divine love—points to you and says, "Mine!"

Grace and peace,
Pastor Eric

GOVERNOR

I shall govern peoples, and nations will be subject to me.
WISDOM OF SOLOMON 8:14

I'M WRITING THIS in my study during a power outage. There was an unhappy car-versus-utility-pole meeting early this morning, and I am watching the good folks from Avista doing the repair work across the street from the church. Fortunately, it's a warm, sunny day, and the battery in my laptop has a good charge, so I can cobble some words together for this monthly missive without any serious discomfort or inconvenience.

Observation: What's different from normal is that I'm facing fewer distractions. No electricity means no phones, which also means no internet service, which means no email or World Wide Sink Hole, which means fewer reasons to multitask and procrastinate. I almost always like it when this happens. Once I finally settle in to this darker, quieter environment, I enjoy the slower pace, along with my new-found ability to stay focused on one thing at a time.

For all of the technological gifts and advances that come from modernity—making our work more productive and our lives more efficient—it is accompanied by collateral damage to our souls. And souls require, among other things, solitude and beauty in order to flourish. My favorite nature theologian, John Muir, famously said, "Thousands of tired, nerve-shaken, over-civilized people are beginning to find out that going to the mountains is going home; that wildness is a necessity."[2]

Observation: Here's something I've grown to notice about myself: I have a built-in anxiety barometer that I have learned to pay attention to. The barometer shows up in the form of a particular song from my childhood. "Gonna jump down, spin around, pick a bale of cotton. Jump down spin around, pick a bale of day. Oh, lordy, pick a bale of cotton. Oh, lordy, pick a bale a day."[3] Depending on my level of anxiety, the song will repeat in my head, increasing in tempo. Silly, I know. Perhaps even pathological. But it is an accurate barometer to measure my anxiety and a dependable indicator that my crowded, noisy soul needs to be reclaimed for holiness.

I spent the summer of my twenty-first year logging forty thousand miles behind the wheel of a Greyhound bus. During my training, I learned that it was equipped with a governor that limited the engine speed and therefore the ground speed. The governor restricted both the engine's revolutions per minute and the bus's miles per hour. Sometimes this was frustrating, like when I was late for a pickup, but it prevented me from getting a speeding ticket, and it made for a longer-lasting engine.

I was familiar with governors because I used to tinker with small engines as a teenager. One spring, when the grass had grown so tall that it was almost impossible to mow, I disabled the governor on a lawn mower and was immediately impressed by how much more power it had. I was pretty impressed with myself as well, for my ability to get more work out of that little engine. That is, until the piston rod broke and destroyed it.

Observation: I have a growing pastoral concern that we have adopted lifestyles that exceed the specifications for which we were designed. We squeeze in more work and play by lengthening our days and shortening our nights. We consume stimulants, and we ignore sabbath. In a variety of ways, we tinker with our God-given governors that keep us from "throwing a rod." Many a hospital visit I've made has revealed to me that we remove these governors to our peril.

There is a singular Governor for our souls who travels through this world at the modest pace of a pedestrian. (Have you ever noticed that the Gospels never show Jesus moving any faster than a walk?) To walk the Jesus way means allowing him to govern our ambitions, our schedules, even our speed, taking great care not to outpace him.

Grace and peace,
Pastor Eric

GEOGRAPHY MATTERS

I like to see a man proud of the place in which he lives. I like to see a man live so that his place will be proud of him.
ABRAHAM LINCOLN

IN PREPARATION for an upcoming trip to England this summer, I recently checked the expiration date on my passport. Passports, as you know, identify us as citizens of the USA and allow us to travel to other parts of the world as temporary guests. Even though I'll be touring in London and studying in Cambridge, my citizenship will remain in the United States. It's my place.

When it comes to our local churches, there are basically three derivations for the names we give them: chronological, theological, or geographical (e.g., First Presbyterian Church, Grace Presbyterian Church, Colbert Presbyterian Church). Each of them carries with it a unique emphasis—namely, when, what, or where—and implicitly suggests which of those identifiers is of greatest importance. To wit, being in order, being orthodox, or being in a place.

Significantly, of the baker's dozen of churches named in the New Testament, each of them is identified by the city they were located in. Within the canon, we have letters written to the churches in Rome, Corinth, Galatia, Ephesus, Philippi, Colossae, Thessalonica, Smyrna, Pergamum, Thyatira, Sardis, Philadelphia, and Laodicea. If you study these letters carefully, you'll see that, while there are some common themes among them all, the authors address something unique to each of them, according to the issues they were facing in their place at the time.

Place is important, because each place is unique. Life on the summit of Mount Everest is dramatically different from life along the Dead Sea. The difference in elevation is 30,340 feet from one extreme to the other, but the differences in life and lifestyles from one altitude to the other, as well as everywhere in between on the map, is endlessly unique. Geography matters.

Over and against a variety of ultraspiritual, antimaterial forms of Gnosticism, the gospel insists that it is the particularities of time, place, and people that make up the context Christ inhabits day in and day out. We are met, saved, and transformed, in other words, according to our unique zip code.

Located in a weirdly shaped geographical area known to the US Postal Service as 99005, Colbert Presbyterian is the place to which we are gathered and formed. But because it's more than a static point on the map, it's also the place from which we are sent into the mission of God. The stability of a parcel of land, in other words, is the anchor point from which we live out the dynamics of a baptized life that sends us "into all the world."[4]

I love the story of Louis IX, king of France, who ruled from 1226 to 1270. When asked why he used to sign his official documents not "King Louis IX," but "Louis of Poissy," he said, "Poissy is the place where I was baptized. I think more of the place where I was baptized than of Rheims Cathedral where I was crowned. It is a greater thing to be a child of God than to be the ruler of a kingdom. This last I shall lose at death, but the other will be my passport to an everlasting glory."[5] You can find those words carved into the stone baptismal font of the church named after him in Cleveland Heights.

Your baptismal identity is what confers upon you your citizenship to the Kingdom of Heaven. It locates you in the vast geography of the Kingdom of God. As aliens in a strange land, it is what assures you of your true and eternal home—your passport, as it were, into heaven. And while it requires daily renewal through our turning from sin and turning to Christ, it bears no expiration date. It's valid until we are, at long last, welcomed to a place called home.

Grace and peace,
Pastor Eric

DUAL CITIZENSHIP

But our citizenship is in heaven, and it is from there that we are expecting a Savior . . .
PHILIPPIANS 3:20

When John the Baptist first announced that the Kingdom of God was at hand, and as Jesus went on to confirm that the Kingdom was, truly, very near, it raised a host of questions for people about where to lodge their loyalty. However, they weren't exactly new questions. Jews at the time were long-accustomed to the tension of living under hostile secular rule (most notably the Egyptian, Babylonian, and Roman empires), while simultaneously embracing their identity and higher calling as the "priestly kingdom and . . . holy nation" of Israel.[6] This often led, as you can imagine, to an awkward dance of allegiances and responsibilities: Is my devotion directed toward the human king or the heavenly one? Daniel, as one notable example, refused to worship King Darius, under penalty of being thrown to the lions. It's always been this way for the chosen people of God as they navigate their uneasy relationship between the Kingdom of God and the various kingdoms of this world. How is one to be "in the world, but not of it"?

Some Christians, relying on James's understanding of true religion as defined by "keeping oneself unstained by the world," assume a posture of distance, if not outright separation from society. Famous among these separatist groups are the Puritans and the Amish.

Yet, when Jesus said that we are salt and light, he was calling us to be seasoning for an otherwise bland world, luminaries in an otherwise dark world. He didn't come to take us out of the world, but rather invites us to enter it and engage it as he does: As God sent the Son into the world, so the Son sends us into the world.[7] The thorny part is being *in* the world in such a way that we do not become *like* the world. Instead of conforming to the values of the world, our calling is to maintain a holy distinctiveness through a unique lifestyle of service in accordance with the values of God's Kingdom. We are sent into the world as little Christs, inviting others to follow him.

We have a foot in each kingdom, but our weight is decidedly shifted toward the Kingdom of Heaven. Because the values of these two kingdoms frequently clash, the church has found it necessary to repeatedly establish its primary allegiance to God's Kingdom in order to maintain its prophetic voice. This is, by the way, why we don't display the American flag in our sanctuary. While we want to be good citizens of our country, obedient to the civil magistrates, and involved in civic matters, our primary allegiance is to Christ. Let there be no confusion or conflation regarding the ultimate object of our fidelity.

My government-issued passport identifies me as a proud US citizen—an identity I will enjoy for a total of about ninety years, if all goes well. My baptismal certificate identifies me as an adopted child of God, a citizen of the never-ending Kingdom of Heaven. The first I carry with me whenever I travel outside the country. The latter is my eternal passport, carrying me into eternity. This is the nature of our dual citizenship. We were born on earth. We were made for heaven.

Grace and peace,
Pastor Eric

BEAUTY IN BROKENNESS

I have become like a broken vessel.

PSALM 31:12

WE KNOW THIS: According to the living systems theory, every living thing—from simple organisms to complex bodies—will experience trauma. No one gets to live for very long without incurring injury of some kind. Bodies, minds, and spirits alike get distorted from their original, pristine condition due to injurious intrusions. The years of our lives add up, accumulating damage of various kinds. For example:

- Damage from the sun creates wrinkles.
- Damage from wounds leaves scars.
- Damage from pregnancy causes stretch marks.
- Damage from betrayal distorts psyches.

Simply stated, it is impossible to go through life without being damaged. There isn't anything or anyone that is able to maintain its original state of goodness and blessing for long.

Additionally, we know that there are one of three possible outcomes to living organisms when they are afflicted.

1. They may die.
2. They may become chronically compromised, limping through the remainder of their life.
3. They may become strengthened precisely at the point of injury.

To some significant degree, any one of those outcomes is due to a decision that gets made somewhere along the way. Give up and roll over, and you die. Become bitter and resentful, and play the part of the victim, and you limp. But choose to cooperate with a redemptive outcome, practice forgiveness, and give yourself to the work of healing, and odds are heavily in your favor that you will become a stronger person. You will grow. You will prove Hemingway right: "The world breaks everyone and afterwards many are strong at the broken places."[8]

You, as I, have probably known people who represent each of those potential outcomes. Without fail, I find that the most joy-filled, wholehearted people I know have at least one chapter of pain in their history. They suffered greatly. And the suffering enlarged their soul. And because they cooperated with the work of redemption, they healed. And in their healing, they were met with a newfound joy. How I want to be *that* kind of person.

There is an ancient Japanese art form that provides a

potent metaphor. Known as *kintsugi*, the technique involves filling the cracks of broken pottery with gold. The result is not only the restoration of functionality, but—more importantly—the creation of beauty. You see, in the absence of damage, there can be no art. It is only because of the brokenness that the beauty can be revealed.

While we live in a world that relentlessly inflicts damage, it is also a world that is occupied by a Redeemer. Therefore, we can participate in the making of art and beauty by embracing brokenness. For those who wait upon the Lord, the broken vessels of Psalm 31 give way to the hope of Psalm 147:3: "He heals the brokenhearted, and binds up their wounds."

There is no damage that is not redeemable, not when it is subject to the grace of God. Therefore, whatever you encounter in this new year, choose the way of life, the way of joy, offering your brokenness to the way of redemption. Do this, and you will be a living exhibit of the Master Artist, adding to the beauty.[9]

Grace and peace,
Pastor Eric

IMPRESSIONS

It belongs to every large nature, when it is not under the immediate power of some strong unquestioning emotion, to suspect itself, and doubt the truth of its own impressions, conscious of possibilities beyond its own horizon.

GEORGE ELIOT, *Romola*

WE ARE IMPRESSIONABLE PEOPLE. Speaking for myself, it's almost embarrassing when I catch myself picking up and mimicking the cadence of the voice of someone I greatly admire. Or when I wake up to a song on my alarm clock radio and it gets stuck in my head throughout the morning. Speaking for someone else, a friend of mine once confessed to me that he's so impressionable that when he goes to see a Western movie, he comes out of the theater walking bowlegged.

Most anything we expose ourselves to and spend time with is bound to affect us in some way. Whether they are first impressions, false impressions, good or bad impressions, we are continually being changed by our environment. Psychologists sometimes refer to it simply as the power of suggestion. Step into a room full of yawning people, and you'll have to work hard to keep yourself from yawning. Advertisers have figured this out and have created a multibillion-dollar industry for the purpose of influencing our spending habits.

That is why, of course, it is important to take care as to whom and by what we allow ourselves to be exposed, for good and for evil. For example, I have found that I am impressed by certain people (Gandhi, Tutu, Teresa, and King come to mind); by certain geological formations (Mount Rainier and Glacier Park stand out); by the power of words as expressed in transcendent poetry (Gerard Manley Hopkins is far and away my favorite); and by the movements of ballet, symphony, and tidal rhythms, to mention but a few of the more positive examples.

I have also learned that I need to be wary, for there is much in this life that opposes the ways of God and which defies the agenda of our souls, which is to grow in holiness. For me, a big part of maturing in Christ has been a matter of guarding my heart, protecting my child-of-God nature, and insulating myself from any influences that might have a corrosive effect on my *imago Dei*. I therefore use care when deciding what books to read, which television and radio broadcasts to take in, what websites to browse, and what people with whom to keep company.

This, of course, is baptism's two-step dance: learning when to say no and when to say yes. No to sin, yes to Christ. Deciding against those influences which work against sanctification and choosing the things that lead me deeper into discipleship. It is a dance which requires our participation and our cooperation. And it is a dance which demands a certain level of vigilance, for evil is forever trying to cut in, or to step on our toes and make us stumble.

I am persuaded that worship is the single most effective experience for reconditioning our hearts into the new creation that God intends to make us. Other practices like personal prayer, Scripture reading, and fellowship are important as well, but worship is the environment where we are assembled as the body of Christ for the purpose of encountering the living God and for training in righteousness. It is where we learn to receive and to convey grace and truth, where we engage the hard work of love, and where we submit ourselves to the care and the discipline of almighty God.

So, remember the sabbath day, and keep it holy. Come and worship. Obey the command, and heed the invitation. You will most certainly be impressed.

Grace and peace,
Pastor Eric

PATIENCE

Rivers know this: There is no hurry. We shall get there some day.

ATTRIBUTED TO WINNIE-THE-POOH

THE TWIN ENEMIES OF THE SOUL are laziness and busyness; succumbing to either is equally deadly. Locating our lives, instead, in that holy-yet-delicate tension between leisureliness and productivity is one of the great challenges of living a good life. However, in the push-pull relationship between doing and being, most of us are pushing to move harder, faster, more efficiently in order to accomplish better and greater things. Whatever goal we consider worthy of pursuit, we go after it in a hurry. And while the culture in which we live tends to reward such efforts and achievements, reinforcing our already-too-busy lives, it often takes its toll in damaging ways. I, therefore, commend to you the virtue of patience.

Not to be confused with laziness, apathy, or underachievement, patience liberates us from the demands for instant results and establishes us in the steadfast love of God, which is as dependable as the tide. Through the years, in the ebb and flow of life, whether things are blessed or bleak, there is no need to panic, no reason to worry. "All things," eventually, "work together for good."[10] The patient way is God's way.

Instead of being defined by daily quotas (how many "to-dos" did you check off your list today?), instead of succumbing to the expectations for quick responses (how many electronic messages did you reply to within a few hours of receiving them?), instead of grabbing our meals on the run and existing on diets of fast food (when was the last time you made a good, home-cooked meal from scratch as a communal event?), patience takes in the long, slow view. It's the perspective of the Kingdom of God in which there are no shortcuts, and detours are simply a part of the journey, since, from God's angle, a thousand years is like a single day.[11] Talk about the patient, long view!

Unfortunately, the notion of patience has become so foreign to our lifestyles that its virtue has actually become confused as a vice. We would do well to recover it for the essential gift that it is. The church fathers considered patience to be chief among the qualities that characterized one's life in Christ. Their ancient wisdom is a reminder that an improved future follows an informed past.

The first three centuries of the church involved a host of challenges and problems. There were conflicts, controversies, heresies, and a variety of hostile forces that sought to undermine the faith of the early Christians, sowing discouragement and even threatening the very existence of the fledgling church. And yet, rather than muscling their way through these obstacles, the bishops called people to steadily stay the course.

From Tertullian, Cyprian, and Lactantius in North Africa, and Justin in Rome, to Clement and Origen in Alexandria, these wise fathers of the church commended patience as the primary character quality that most distinguished Christians in the world. I especially like how Cyprian put it: "Nothing else distinguishes the unjust from the just more than this, that in adversities the unjust man complains and blasphemes because of impatience, while the just man is proved by patience."[12]

The New Testament—itself a slowly gathered compilation of stories and letters—has frequent references to the importance of living a patient faith. Saint Paul, for example, includes patience, along with love, joy, and peace in the good company of the fruits of the Spirit,[13] those qualities that are exhibited by people in whom the Holy Spirit dwells. And when he seeks to show us the "more excellent way" of love he begins by saying that "love is *patient*."[14]

Christians are patient people living in an impatient world, exercising restraint, demonstrating forbearance, practicing tolerance, trusting that the Kingdom of God is among us and that the promises of God are being fulfilled in God's sweet time. In our hyperbusy world, this may be the virtue we need most to recover, the one which has the capacity to slow us down to the speed of God, thereby serving the agenda of our souls, as well as the characteristic that distinguishes the people of God from the rest of the world. Follow the patient way. Practice this way. It's the way of Jesus.

Grace and peace,
Pastor Eric

FORMATION

Most middle-class Americans tend to worship their work, work at their play, and play at their worship.

GORDON DAHL,

Work, Play, and Worship in a Leisure-Oriented Society

TO BE ALIVE is to be in a state of constant change. We are ever on the move, sometimes sprinting toward life, other times shuffling toward death. We can see it at the biological level as our cells come and go, multiplying one moment, sloughing off in another. Moreover, such change occurs at the level of consciousness where awareness ebbs and flows as knowledge is gained and information is forgotten. To be human is to carry the effects of both life and death in our very bodies.

To be alive in Christ, similarly, involves such gains and losses, mostly related directly to our baptismal affirmations and renunciations: We turn to Jesus as we simultaneously turn from sin and evil. We nurture the fruits of the Spirit as we forsake the works of the flesh. Over the course of a lifetime, these accompanying choices and lifestyle patterns change us, for good or for bad. Which is to say, we can either cooperate with or defy the agenda for holiness.

As a pastor entrusted with the care and the cure of souls, I am primarily interested in helping you grow to become mature, "to the measure of the full stature of Christ."[15] This, I believe, is the high standard by which I will be judged. However, it is a work that is fraught with many challenges because the culture we live in poses a host of compelling and competing alternatives that are frequently considered to be more attractive. Never before have we had such a flood of choices available to us with respect to how we should direct (not *spend*; we are trustees of resources, not consumers) our time, our money, our attention, our love.

Far too often, with so many more exciting, head-turning options available, God gets little more than a nod. The result of giving to God our leftovers rather than our "firstfruits" is shriveling souls, and it's often too late before we even realize how diminished we've become over time. Lifestyle patterns and practices reflect the values we hold dear; they not only reveal what we love but they affect the kinds of people we are becoming. It's never been more important for us or for our children to be choosy as we are being fit for citizenship in the Kingdom of God.

Therefore, I solemnly urge you to recommit yourself to the holy observance of sabbath-keeping as we enter this new academic year. Establish yourself in this practice of *becoming* through weekly worship and the daily disciplines related to Scripture, prayer, and service. These are the holy patterns which effectively form us in godliness over the course of a lifetime. It all adds up, so that we can grow to measure up to "the full stature of Christ."

Grace and peace,
Pastor Eric

SABBATH

Stop for one whole day every week, and you will remember what it means to be created in the image of God, who rested on the seventh day not from weariness but from complete freedom. The clear promise is that those who rest like God find themselves free like God, no longer slaves to the thousand compulsions that send others rushing toward their graves.

BARBARA BROWN TAYLOR, *Leaving Church*

CALL ME OLD-FASHIONED, but there are some things in the Bible that I don't believe we will ever be able to dismiss or relegate to "cultural" or "time-bound" issues the way we have, for example, come (and rightly so, I believe) to new understandings of the Levitical dietary laws or the role of women in leadership. Among the Scriptures where there is very little, if any, "wiggle room" is the rock-solid nature of the Ten Commandments. They are just as true, just as timely, and just as necessary in our day as the day Moses brought them down from the smoky summit of Mount Sinai. And yet in our day, some of them are largely ignored and flat-out disobeyed, perhaps none of them more so than the fourth commandment, the one that has the longest commentary of any of the other nine. Here it is in its entirety:

> Remember the sabbath day, and keep it holy. Six days you shall labor and do all your work. But the seventh day is a sabbath to the LORD your God; you shall not do any work—you, your son or your daughter, your male or female slave, your livestock, or the alien resident in your towns. For in six days the LORD made heaven and earth, the sea, and all that is in them, but rested the seventh day; therefore the LORD blessed the sabbath day and consecrated it.
> EXODUS 20:8-11

Interestingly, the version recorded in Deuteronomy 5:15 is quite similar, but with this one significant addition:

> Remember that you were a slave in the land of Egypt, and the LORD your God brought you out from there with a mighty hand and an outstretched arm; therefore the LORD your God commanded you to keep the sabbath day.

The implication is that while work is inherently good and godly, work can also put us back into bondage if it begins to define and dominate our lives. When that happens, we become slaves to work, losing our freedom and robbing ourselves of the abundance and joy that God longs for us to experience. Be clear about this: We do it to ourselves, with no evil "masters"—Egyptian, American, political, corporate, or otherwise—to blame.

Still, many of us cling to an extreme work ethic almost as a badge of honor, complaining in thinly disguised phrases of self-congratulation (sometimes accompanied by dramatic sighs for added emphasis): "I'm just so busy" or "he works so hard" or "she hasn't had a day off in weeks."

When I hear such things, I assume that people are confessing their sins to me. Overwork is not virtuous, and it's not holy. You might be earning the admiration of other people who have lost their selves as slaves to work, but you're not impressing God. It's sin.

We have simply got to get over the false notion of associating a day of rest with being lazy, or the idea that being nonproductive for a day makes us worthless. Rather, a recovery of sabbath-keeping, sabbath-remembering practices may be the very antidote to our harried lives which have become distorted by a Protestant work ethic juiced with the steroids of ambition, the drive for success, and the need to impress.

This lifelong process of becoming godly requires that we think and behave more and more like God. Recover for yourself the *imago Dei* by doing what God does. Give it a rest. Live free. God commands it. Your baptism demands it. Your soul needs it.

Grace and peace,
Pastor Eric

TIME IN THE WOMB

Lend me, therefore, O Baptist, your right hand for the present economy, even as Mary lent her womb for my birth.
PSEUDO-GREGORY THAUMATURGUS

It's no secret that I love children. At every developmental stage, I remain endlessly enthralled and entertained by their innocence, their curiosity, and their ability to teach and delight. The accompanying antics and unruliness that sometimes interrupt the pleasure they give me are but a small (and sometimes hilarious) price to pay for the gifts they bring. My life would be immeasurably impoverished without children.

It's no surprise that Jesus loved children. There were just a few things that could ignite the indignation of his otherwise peaceful demeanor: not practicing what you preach (hypocrisy), using the house of worship for financial gain (exploitation), and refusing to repent (stubbornness).[16] However, the strongest language of his we have recorded was reserved for those who dared to harm a child: "It would be better for you if a millstone were hung around your neck and you were thrown into the sea than for you to cause one of these little ones to stumble."[17]

And so, it's no surprise that Jesus not only welcomed children into his arms so that he could bless them but also called for the adults around him to be more like them: "Unless you change and become like children, you will never enter the kingdom of heaven."[18] How odd those words must have sounded to those who first heard them! To some of us they still do. But what at first sounds like going backward is actually the only holy way forward.

Christian maturation, or what Paul described as growing up "to the measure of the full stature of Christ" is not the same thing as getting old. As our years add up, there are many aspects of our childhood that we grow out of, and rightly so. However, there are some childlike qualities that, when retained, fit us more fully for the Kingdom of God. Vulnerability—a distinctively childlike trait—may be chief among them.

Children *believe* before they *know* much of anything. They believe they are loved, that their needs are worth meeting, and that their parents will attend them, provide for them, and keep them safe. When those beliefs are met by parental fidelity, the reliance children have on their caregivers creates a profound bond of trust and of love. Just so, such childlike vulnerability and trusting behavior toward our heavenly Father is the entry point to the Kingdom, as well as the way of deepening intimacy with the Lover of our soul.

Perhaps this is why Jesus told a fully grown-up man one

night that he must be "born anew." As with anybody who takes his words too literally, Nicodemus missed the meaning of the metaphor, imagining himself crawling back inside his mother's uterus. But Jesus made himself clear: "No one can enter the kingdom of God without being born of water and Spirit."[19] This is how we begin our new life in Christ and grow to become increasingly like Christ: wet and winded.

Advent annually extends the invitation to return to the womb of rebirth, to renew our spirits, to be born anew. Unfortunately, our seasonal surroundings, with their increased activities, noise, and lights, don't lend to the quiet, dark, fertile conditions needed for the new-life rebeginnings our souls require, and so it's important to seek out womb-like environments in which we can gestate and grow. This is the silent gift and the hidden work of Advent, that we might more fully become who we already are: "'children of God.' And that's only the beginning. Who knows how we'll end up!"[20]

Grace and peace,
Pastor Eric

PRESENT-FUTURE

View the present through the promise, Christ will come again.
THOMAS TROEGER, "View the Present through the Promise"

WE ALL HAVE OUR BIASES and prejudices that reflect our personalities, our preferences, our assumptions, and our worldviews. For example, the fact that I am a white, Anglo-Saxon, Protestant, North American male of Scandinavian descent affects my perspective on just about everything, from my understanding of power to my love of potatoes. My Myers-Briggs Type Indicator (INFP) is one way to understand my preferred way of relating to the world and to individuals.

The so-called bandwagon effect is one of the more well-known biases that occur in society, referring to the phenomenon that people do certain things because other people are doing them. We are—all of us—more biased than we know, sometimes mistaking mere preferences for dogmatic convictions. Mature and self-aware people, recognizing these biases at work in themselves, seek to intentionally step away from them from time to time, knowing that theirs is not the only way, and often not the best way, to see or understand an issue.

Because of their prevailing nature, these biases are continually at work, affecting even the way we read the Scriptures. A wealthy American, for example, reads and understands the Bible quite differently from a poor person living in a Guatemalan barrio in the wake of war. The person who adopts bumper-sticker philosophies like "God said it. I believe it. That settles it." assumes that her way is the only way to understand Scripture, when, in reality, there is no pure way to read God's Word; it comes to us through our own biased filters.

We can also *impose* a bias on a text. In biblical studies, we call this a hermeneutic—a lens through which the Scriptures are read. In recent years, it has been popular to explore hermeneutics of liberation and feminism, to name but two among many. Such lenses can help us to pay attention to issues of human oppression, in order to help us participate more meaningfully in acts of justice.

Our biases, biblical and otherwise, influence the ways we think about and live our lives. They are the source of fundamental personal defaults like optimism or pessimism, hope or dread, peace or anxiety, courage or fear, abundance or scarcity. By noticing when our inclinations tip away from what we might call "Kingdom values," we can make some course corrections to our lives, adjusting our perspective and adopting a new bias.

These remaining days of Lent extend just such an invitation for self-reflection and repentance, examining the ways our lives have gotten off the holy track of discipleship, and then doing whatever (yes, what*ever!*) is necessary to get right. I have found it helpful, in my own pursuit of holiness, to nurture a hermeneutic of Resurrection. Such a bias, I am finding, deeply influences all the aspects of the essential me, including such things as attitude, relationships, work, and faith that are in need of godly influences in order for me to grow in Christlikeness.

We live the present complete with all the problems and heartaches that assail us because we live in a fearful and broken world. We need to learn to deal with that. But we also lean into the hope of a future where sin is dealt a definitive blow when Christ comes again and presides over the consummation of God's redemptive promises. "We are," as someone once said, "an Easter people living in a Good Friday world."[21]

Apply a Resurrection hermeneutic to your life, living fully in the present through the promise that Christ will come again. It changes everything.

Grace and peace,
Pastor Eric

PRAYER 101

Hannah was praying silently; only her lips moved, but her voice was not heard.
1 SAMUEL 1:13

I'M STUCK in the kindergarten of prayer. Many times my prayers, if you were to overhear them, sound inarticulate, scattered, incoherent. They are the blurted-out blatherings of a soul who is frequently caught speechless, the clumsy meanderings of my disordered desires. Typically, my private prayers are barely audible, unrehearsed sighs.

That's not necessarily an admission of my deficiencies. I learned a lot of things in kindergarten that formed me into the person I am today. They are things that remain good, and true, and right, and things, therefore, that I need to come back to from time to time. For example, it was in Mrs. Paige's class where I first learned the alphabet, where I was taught to share and to take turns, and where I memorized my home address. I even remember an occasion on the playground when she made me repeat after her as she instructed me in the art of offering a genuine apology to a classmate I had offended. I don't recall the offense I committed, but I do remember the apology these many years later. It was all pretty simple, yet enormously important stuff I learned in my kindergarten year from a kind, strong, black woman who had a voice like honey.

We live our lives from a foundation of fundamentals. And whenever our lives become disoriented, it is helpful to become reacquainted with the basics in order to be reestablished in our identity and purpose.

Prayer is the foundational language of faith. And prayer, I have learned, is best when it emerges from and is built on a simple foundation. Following is my understanding of the three most fundamental types of prayer, the basis of a meaningful faith (which leads to a meaningful life), accompanied by some brief reflections that I hope will prompt further consideration.

Lord, have mercy. Much of life is out of our control. Even the most self-sufficient people among us experience challenges beyond their capacity to handle. When the storms of trouble crash in, overwhelming our competencies, we have a choice to either wring our hands in worry or fold our hands in humility; we can either panic or we can pray. This is the ancient prayer that first reminds us of our frailty and our mortality and then locates us in the strength and everlasting nature of our God, who is limitless in love, and whose mercy never quits: *kyrie eleison.*

Thank you, Jesus. Gratitude is the hallmark of the Christian life. In recognition that we live in a world full of gifts, that, indeed, all of life is a gift, we turn to the source of all good things and sing, "Praise God from whom all blessings flow."

Like the one among ten lepers who was healed, we take the time to turn back, and say, "Thanks!" Recognizing that the goodness of life could be otherwise, we don't take the gifts for granted but rather express our gratitude. It's difficult to squander gifts, and even harder to succumb to spiritual amnesia when living doxologically.

Here I am. Inexplicably, for all the ways God could redeem this old world so much more effectively on his own, he continues to prefer to work through human agency to accomplish his holy purposes. A meaningful life begins in a posture of readiness, making ourselves available to the God who calls and commissions willing people, as we echo Isaiah: "Here am I, send me!"[22]

Lord, have mercy. Thank you, Jesus. Here I am. Sometimes we specialize in one of these three prayers during a particular season of life. Other times we may offer all three of them in a single day. Either way, practicing these simple prayers over a lifetime is among the formative behaviors which fit us for the Kingdom of God.

It just now occurs to me that as I write this, I am preparing to attend a graduation ceremony at George Fox University, a reminder that, while I am now a doctor of the church, when it comes to prayer, I am no more sophisticated than a kindergartener. And that, I believe, is a good thing.

Grace and peace,
Pastor Eric

DISCERNING THE VOICES

Prepare our hearts, O Lord, to accept your word. Silence in us any voice but your own, that, hearing, we may also obey your will; through Jesus Christ our Lord. Amen.

THE WORSHIPBOOK OF THE PRESBYTERIAN CHURCH

THAT PRAYER, which comes from the old Book of Common Worship, is the prayer that I heard every Sunday for nineteen years as I was growing up in my home church in Bel Air, Maryland. Christ Our King Presbyterian, like Colbert Presbyterian, is located on the corner of a busy highway. The church of my adulthood is at the intersection of Highway 2 and Colbert Road. The church of my childhood can be found at the corner of Route 924 and Lexington Road. The obvious things those two churches have in common? They are Presbyterian; the organizing pastors were Petersons; and this prayer: "Prepare our hearts, O Lord, to accept your word. Silence in us any voice but your own, that, hearing, we may also obey your will." Though you might initially assume that it's a prayer for people suffering from schizophrenia, it's known as the prayer for illumination, and it was always offered right before the sermon was preached.

Being a fourth-generation pastor, you could say that serving you as a minister of Word and Sacrament is an indication that I went into the family business. On both sides of my family tree, there have been and are pastors and missionaries, in the form of both Pentecostals and Presbyterians who have served from Osaka, Japan, to Omak, Washington. But in each case, they are members of an extended family of men and women who have been called to proclaim the Word of God.

In ways that I don't fully understand, I represent a continuation of ministry that has been taking place on both sides of my biological and spiritual gene pool for many years. I am the person and the pastor I am today because I am an heir to a rich spiritual legacy. The gift of that legacy has also been tempered by some unique challenges, particularly as I have struggled to find my own voice rather than simply to mimic the voices I have grown up with and around. I've worked hard over the last twenty-seven years to differentiate my own voice from the pastoral voices of my great-grandfather, my grandmother, my three uncles, my two cousins, and my dad.

But every Sunday morning, there is a moment that represents a continuation of my father's voice: this prayer of illumination, offered on behalf of his congregation for twenty-nine consecutive years, a prayer that gradually and quietly worked its way into my imagination and which has been a consistent part of our liturgy here for the past twenty years. "Silence in us any voice but your own."

The prayer betrays the assumption that there are many voices that reach our ears, some more appealing than others, and often in competition with one another, contradicting each other. We come to worship week after week seeking God, hungering for a word from the Lord, while accompanied by the din of other voices telling us who we are, what we should do, what's really important. A lot of voices vying for our attention, courting our allegiance, imposing demands. Lots of voices. And they threaten, at times, to crowd out the voice of God. They are sometimes even loud enough to speak over a word from the Lord. And so we pray, "Silence in us any voice but your own."

From the baptismal waters of the Jordan to the arid scabland of the wilderness, Jesus heard the same voices we all hear: a word from heaven; a word from hell. The voice of God; the voice of Satan. A word of pleasure; a word of enticement. A word to build up; a word to destroy. And it's not always easy to tell the difference, especially when the satanic words are dressed in holy clothing, in the very words of Scripture. The voices we hear, the messages we receive don't have to sound evil in an obvious kind of way in order to truly be diabolical. Just as wolves sometimes appear in sheep's clothing, so, too, Satan can speak in the voice of an angel. Which means this life of following Jesus can be a little prickly if we're not paying attention, if we're not prayerfully discerning the voices, by foremost becoming familiar with the voice of God.

Grace and peace,
Pastor Eric

ADVENT AMBIVALENCE

How can this be, since I am a virgin?
LUKE 1:34

I've been hearing the phrase more frequently lately. People describe their position on a particular topic and then attempt to reinforce it by saying something like, "Scripture is clear on this issue." Whenever I hear it, more often than not, an internal voice of mine responds with, *Really? I've been studying the Scriptures for many years, and I don't think the biblical witness on that subject is at all clear. Or if it looks clear in one place, you can find an opposing view elsewhere.* The Ten Commandments are the notable exception to my observation that most Scripture needs to be interpreted carefully and respectfully if we are to avoid rigid, narrow, and dogmatic "positions" in favor of maintaining Christ-honoring relationships with one another through godly conversation.

The bumper sticker I once saw seems to capture the spirit of the person who has no room in their lives for nuance and ambiguity: "God said it. I believe it. That settles it." Such a statement, while attractive to those who value decisiveness and conviction, especially when it comes to moral clarity, leaves one wondering if everything is as black and white as might be hoped. I wonder sometimes where this desire for crystal clarity comes from. Why do we find it important, necessary, or even attractive to be so sure about so many things?

Ambivalence is a phenomenon that shows up rather consistently in the biblical narrative. I think, for example, of the times when the angel Gabriel visited Zechariah and Mary, in turn, with the news that they would become parents. Both of them, in their own way, seemed to struggle with the birth announcement: Zechariah because he and his wife were too old, and Mary because she was too young, and chaste. Clearly, people in such conditions do not procreate. But each of them learned to embrace the promise by first embracing their own ambivalence. "How will I know that this is so?" Zechariah asked, "For I am an old man, and my wife is getting on in years."[23] "How can this be?" asked Mary, "since I am a virgin?" They had their questions, like any thinking person would. Some things just don't make sense at the time.

Certain seasons of our lives can create these feelings of ambivalence as well. Almost always, they occur during a transition of some kind: in between jobs, in between relationships, and in between homes are a few of the typical ones. And it is this "in-betweenness"—the ending of one thing and the beginning of another, when the end isn't quite finished and the beginning hasn't quite arrived—that often creates the uncomfortable experience of having mixed or confusing feelings about something or someone.

A helpful image given to me, while living through a painful season of transition myself, was that of a trapeze. Picture, if you will, three main stages represented in the metaphor: hanging on to a trapeze bar, flying in midair, grabbing hold of the next trapeze bar. That period of time when we are in between, hovering in midair, with nothing solid to hang on to, is a time of uncertainty and fear, and most people have difficulty managing their anxiety in that tentative space for very long. Ambivalence, admittedly, is an uncomfortable place to abide, and we typically push for clarity or resolution of the issues in our lives that remain annoyingly ambiguous. We search desperately for something to "hang on" to.

Our postmodern world, mostly with its technological "advances," offers us many options, ways to move more quickly from one thing to another in order to abbreviate the discomfort of the in-between time. Consider how:

- Transportation is faster and easier.
- Communication is faster and easier.
- Food is faster and easier.
- Information gathering is faster and easier.
- Credit approval is faster and easier.

All of this speed and ease has conditioned us to believe that we shouldn't have to wait for much of anything. If we want it badly enough, we can have it now. In fact, we've been taught to believe that we *deserve* it quickly. We are surrounded by the kind of conveniences that can often make our lives easier but not fuller.

In holy defiance of the cultural frenzy that is enticing us all to amp up activities, and to increase consumption and spending, I invite you this year to observe an Advent that includes the acknowledgement that we are an "in-between people," embracing the reality that there are unrelenting loose ends in our lives and there is chronic unfinished business in the world. Trust me, everything that is important will get resolved in due time by God.

Some things, especially the incomplete things related to the health and vitality of our souls, must be lived with rather than rushed through.

Grace and peace,
Pastor Eric

WALK THE PLANK

If we say we that we have no sin, we deceive ourselves, and the truth is not in us. If we confess our sins, he who is faithful and just will forgive us our sins and cleanse us from all unrighteousness.
I JOHN 1:8-9

PERSUADED THAT THE CHURCH of the twenty-first century will have more in common with the church of the first five centuries than it will with the twentieth century, I have been getting reacquainted with the early church fathers over the last couple of years. To my great pleasure, I have been struck by the way they—to a person—placed a strong emphasis on the importance of baptism, not only the necessity of *getting* wet but the importance of *living* wet. Baptism both marks the *beginning* of our life in Christ and characterizes our lifelong journey of *becoming* like Christ. This is our primary identity: children of God, growing up in Christ. Like children, however, we develop gradually. Abraham-like, we journey by stages.

It didn't take the Fathers any longer than it takes us

to realize that, while the sacrament of baptism represents the washing away of sin, sin persists among the baptized, nonetheless.

Recognizing the ongoing temptations to sin, as well as the reality of actually sliding (or tumbling, as the case may be) into sin, thereby defying the sacred nature of the new covenant, these early church pastors found language which was useful in restoring a person who had strayed from their baptismal moorings. Acknowledging the need for ongoing repentance subsequent to baptism, several of them introduced the wonderful notion of the "second plank."

Tertullian, the early church father who first coined the phrase, suggested that confession of our sin and repentance from our sin is (as Jerome would later put it) "a plank for those who have had the misfortune to be shipwrecked."[24] In his own words (it needs to be read more than once):

> This will draw you forth when sunk in the waves of sins, and it will bear you forward into the port of the divine clemency. Seize the opportunity of unexpected felicity: that you, who sometime were in God's sight nothing but "a drop of a bucket," and "dust of the threshing floor," and "a potter's vessel," may thenceforward become that "tree which is sown beside the waters, is perennial in leaves, bears fruit at its own time," and shall not see "fire," nor "axe." Having found "the truth," repent of errors; repent of having loved what God loves not.[25]

The metaphor—as a sort of makeshift lifeboat in the stormy sea of sin—conjures a compelling image of rescue and forgiveness. While "walking the plank" is now more commonly associated with death by drowning, Tertullian's image of the second plank suggests how repentance is the life preserver that restores people who are thrashing about in the waves of sin to the grace of God's unending mercy. The wet sacrament, of course, captures beautifully both sides of the baptismal coin: the necessity for the old self to be destroyed in order for a new life to be buoyed in Christ.

In our twenty-first-century climate of positivism, we might do well to recover the early church's realism that includes an acknowledgement of sin and evil, along with a way to deal with it, by confessing our sins, renouncing evil, and clinging to Christ. To refuse to offer our prayers of confession to a merciful God is akin to a shipwrecked person not crying out for help when a lifeboat passes by. We don't need to be merely improved; we need to be rescued, and repentance is the lifeline, our salvation-plank from death to life. Walk this way.

Grace and peace,
Pastor Eric

TREASURES OLD AND NEW

Christianity is a progressive enterprise. Our vastly enlarged perspectives of knowledge should open up fresh vistas of religious faith. The Bible . . . may be still pregnant with unsuspected lessons.

MICHAEL POLANYI, *Personal Knowledge*

I'VE BEEN CHEWING on that quote for about three years now. It's still not fully digested in my mind, but it rings true to my (somewhat) sanctified common sense. There was a time when I would have been offended by such a suggestion. During the early developmental years of my faith, I believed that God's truth was absolute, static, and nonnegotiable. I also believed that I had a pretty good grasp on it. Since that time, I have repented of my arrogance more than once.

Because as I got older, I was exposed to perspectives that pointed out the limitations and biases I carry with me due to being a white, Anglo-Saxon, Protestant, middle-class, North American, straight male. I traveled to other parts of the world, read books, and listened to people who were vastly and wonderfully different from me. Gradually—though sometimes rapidly—I realized that my little perch wasn't the only perspective from which to see and comprehend the world.

While studying church history, I came to understand how mainline, orthodox Christianity has, in fact, evolved and progressed, based on new information, and has emerged from careful (not always civil) conversations between people in search of truth. Today I am grateful for the progress that has been made so that the church is no longer condoning things like crusades, indulgences, sexism, misogyny, slavery, and witch hunts. I also wonder what we remain wrong about, in both little and large ways, because to believe that we have arrived at a point of perfection, with a complete grasp of truth, is the height of arrogance.

My own journey of *becoming* has, additionally, been influenced by my observation that the older, wiser people I most admired were people who were always learning, always open to new ideas, eager to grow in their understanding of the complexities of the world and the mysteries of faith. Because of these people, I resolved to be a lifelong learner by approaching life with curiosity and humility.

None of this is to say that all new ideas or trends or practices are necessarily good. Far from it. All new notions should be carefully discerned through the lens of church history, under the authority of the holy Scriptures, and in the context of the Christian community. I have found that John Wesley's quadrilateral made up of Scripture, tradition, reason, and experience is a helpful method for progressing toward truth.

In the newness of a New Year, may we locate our lives

in the steadiness of a time-tested and enduring faith that is as solid as the Rock on which it is founded. And may we be open to the ways the Holy Spirit is enlarging our perspective, correcting our false assumptions, and opening us to fresh vistas of divine truth. May we, in other words, live as those scribes Jesus once commended, people who have been trained for the Kingdom of Heaven, who are "like the master of a household who brings out of his treasure what is new and what is old."[26]

Grace and peace,
Pastor Eric

LENTEN LEFTOVERS

Gather up the fragments left over, so that nothing may be lost.
JOHN 6:12

I GREW UP with a Scotch-Presbyterian mother who threw away very few things. There was a ragbag at the bottom of our basement stairs where old clothes were tossed and made into quilts; we had a compost bin for potato peels and apple cores that eventually made their way into her organic garden; and the kitchen stocked an assortment of Tupperware in which to store all leftovers, from all meals, no matter how small—even something as small as a tablespoon of tomato paste, as I now recall. Without saying a word about it, she taught me both that food was a precious gift and that frugality was a virtue to be honored and practiced: "waste not, want not." Food—I grew up learning—should not be squandered or taken for granted. Consequently, to this day, my favorite lunch is last evening's leftovers.

In the various versions of the miracle commonly known

as the multiplication of loaves and fishes, some of the details vary. Was it four thousand or five thousand people that were fed? Was it five loaves or seven? Two fish or "a few"? It depends on which Gospel account you happen to be reading. However, one of the details that is consistent among all of these reports is that after everyone in the crowd had eaten to their satisfaction, there were a lot of "broken pieces" of food, and Jesus directed his disciples to gather up the leftovers. Again, the accounts vary, but there was anywhere between seven and twelve baskets of leftovers that were saved. The story ends there, leaving me to wonder who benefited from the leftovers of that miraculous two-course miracle.

It causes me to wonder about other kinds of leftovers as well. In a world that is good at hurrying us along to the next big thing, Lent invites us to gather up the fragments of our lives and to linger over them, attending them, even savoring them. Some such fragments may be a mere wisp of a fond memory, while others may be bitter with unresolved conflict. Either way, they are among the parts of our lives that we benefit from by attending to and then offering up to God, who is keen to reclaim our lives by integrating the whole of them into his Kingdom. And God, I am persuaded, wastes nothing; everything, rather, is raw material for redemption.

Recently, as I was listening to someone sharing with me an experience that was accompanied by profound regret, the memory of which she was unable to shrug off, as she was (as we all do) trying to make sense of it and figure out what to do about it, I said, "Do not waste this pain. Something here is demanding your attention. The pain is not to be avoided, but lived, so that you can be healed. You will outlive this pain, and it will eventually serve to enlarge your soul." This is the nature of deep, spiritual work: listening to the small, broken fragments of our lives that don't have a voice of their own. And in listening to the still, small voice of our soul, we hear the voice of God.

There are a lot of broken pieces that make up our lives, and Jesus wants to make sure that none of them are lost. So gather up the scattered pieces—the ruined dreams and the hidden memories, the scars that have healed well along with the wounds which yet bleed—so that nothing is wasted. Lent is a perfect season to gather up the long-neglected leftovers of our lives, to linger over these forgotten fragments and thereby honor the agenda of our hungry hearts.

Grace and peace,
Pastor Eric

GUARDING THE HEART

The heart is devious above all else; it is perverse—who can understand it?
JEREMIAH 17:9

EVEN AT A TIME when there was only a rudimentary understanding of anatomy—from the days of Noah, actually—both the human heart and the heart of God were understood to be something of a locus for feelings and for motivation. When there is sadness, it is the heart that grieves. When there is evil, its source is the heart. People who are strong in character are admired as "stout-hearted," and those who are stubborn are condemned as "hard-hearted." The heart is where pride begins, the place from which joy emerges, and the part of us that allows commitments to be made. In biblical psychology, the heart is the central and unifying organ of a person's life that can be made strong with food and can be made glad with wine. Clearly it is accompanied by literal as well as figurative meanings.

Jesus blessed those who were pure in heart, and he condemned those whose hearts were God-averse. Belief in God, ultimately, is a matter of the heart. The New Testament word is *kardia*, which has worked its way into our language in obvious ways.

Increasingly these days, we are caring for our physical hearts by watching our diet and choosing "heart-healthy menu items," by exercising, and perhaps by taking medication for various heart-related diseases, from high blood pressure to high cholesterol. What an amazing and essential machine the human heart is, pumping every second or so, circulating blood all through our bodies, transporting necessary oxygen and nutrients to every extremity. And when it fails, we quite simply die. Cardiac arrest.

There is an additional aspect of cardio care that we neglect to our peril. Referring to our universal hunger for God, the great fourth-century Catholic Bishop Augustine wrote, "You have made us for yourself, and our heart is restless until it rests in you."[27] Unfortunately, restless hearts don't always find their way to God, at least not entirely. And these divided or homeless hearts of ours can be damaged along the way, compromising our spiritual health, distancing us from God.

One of my growing pastoral concerns is the way that pornographic material can affect, even *infect*, our hearts. Recent studies are showing an alarming and growing trend of pornographic use made more easily accessible through the convenience and the confidentiality of the Internet. Like most other addictions, it can have an insidiously escalating effect with more and more exposure to increasingly explicit material. And as with other addictions, it can spill over into other aspects of life, leading to disastrous results.

But it doesn't have to be this way. Although many temptations are unavoidable and abundant, we always have a choice as to how we are going to respond to them. A growing number of people, acknowledging the vulnerability of their hearts and recognizing the high stakes that are involved, are using filters on their computers. Another way to build in accountability is to subscribe to a service such as CovenantEyes.com, which monitors a person's internet activity, evaluates it for appropriate content, and sends a report to an accountability partner of your choosing. As a pastor, I am always happy to be the recipient of such reports as a way of encouraging people to consistently integrate their faith values with their lifestyle choices. While it may involve relinquishing certain liberties and freedoms, that is sometimes the cost of ensuring safety in a yet fearful and broken world. By voluntarily submitting to a life of transparency, discipline, and accountability, we are actually, paradoxically, able to live lives of greater, more expansive freedom and wholeheartedness in Christ.

So protect your hearts against sin and evil. Be careful what you allow yourself to see and do and think about. Build in safeguards to help you stay accountable for the holy life that God wants for you, and which I truly believe we want for ourselves. Guard your hearts, for nothing less than your very soul is at stake.

Grace and peace,
Pastor Eric

STRETCHING EXERCISES

I stretch out my hands to you;
my soul thirsts for you like a parched land.
PSALM 143:6

THERE IS SOMETHING about being stretched to the limits that has a way of increasing one's capacity. Bend your body toward the floor for a minute every day, and eventually you'll be touching your toes again. Suffer with chronic pain long enough, and your threshold for tolerating the discomfort goes up. Go through a season that is characterized by one challenge after another, stretching you thin—even to the breaking point—and you may be surprised to find that you can handle much more than you ever believed possible. Stretching increases your capacity—body, mind, and spirit.

And since everything—as I have been working hard to convince you for the last twenty years!—has to do with baptism, you will not be surprised to know that the word *fathom*, usually used to refer to a depth of six feet of water, literally means "a stretch of the arms." The baptized way of life plunges us into the deep end of the pool of life, immersing us in circumstances where we frequently find ourselves way over our heads—"out of our depth," as they say. It's not hard to feel overwhelmed, especially when the waves are crashing overhead. Treading these waters, however, strengthens us in ways we couldn't have previously fathomed.

I've been feeling stretched in some new ways recently. It can be a bit uncomfortable at times and is frequently overwhelming; sometimes I wonder if it's sustainable. However, I've been surprised and pleased to discover that, just when I think I'm at my limit, my limitations expand. I call this grace. One of the effects of these stretching days is that my capacity for gratitude has also increased: With few exceptions, I end my days with a word of thanks on my lips. I call this grace as well.

The soul, *your* soul, is endlessly resilient, and it has great capacity for growth during its earthly pilgrimage. At nearly every twist and turn, every bend and break of life, there are plenty of opportunities to exercise our faith. More kinesthetic than sedentary, the life of discipleship moves: we walk, we lean toward heaven, we follow Jesus. Emerging from the pain of life is the miracle that, with every movement we make, with every stretch of faith, we are exercising the fibers that increase our capacity for joy, fitting us for a life as big as the Kingdom of God.

Grace and peace,
Pastor Eric

TE DEUM (WE PRAISE THEE, O GOD)

Grace and gratitude belong together like heaven and earth. Grace evokes gratitude like the voice of an echo. Gratitude follows grace like thunder lightning. . . . We are speaking of the grace of the God who is God for man, and of the gratitude of man as his response to this grace. Here, at any rate, the two belong together, so that only gratitude can correspond to grace, and this correspondence cannot fail.

KARL BARTH, *Church Dogmatics,* IV.1

THE HUMAN SOUL has been masterfully designed with the ability to enlarge endlessly. With divine brilliance, we have been created to grow. Even when our bodies stop growing somewhere in early adulthood, there is other, less visible but no less important growth still occurring. And while it is indeed true that we begin to experience something of a decline in many of our faculties and functions as we tack on birthdays, there is never a shortage of raw material to form us more and more fully in the likeness of Christ.

Most people eventually learn the hard way (which is the only way to learn some things) that sometimes it is the toughest, most painful experiences that end up being the greatest gifts in service to the growth of our souls. While almost always received initially as unwelcome intrusions, these disruptions have a way of teaching and forming us in ways that happy circumstances can't. Saint Paul, no stranger to firsthand pain, the likes of which most of us will never, fortunately, have to experience, knew this to be true, writing:

> We also boast in our sufferings, knowing that suffering produces endurance, and endurance produces character, and character produces hope, and hope does not disappoint us, because God's love has been poured into our hearts through the Holy Spirit that has been given to us.
>
> ROMANS 5:3-5

Endurance. Character. Hope. Love. Those are hard-earned virtues, and you don't have to look very hard to see the scars that accompany them. What suffering people typically learn is that the grace of God gravitates *toward* pain. It is where the Christ, himself well-acquainted with grief, shows up, complete with his own wounds, his own scars, his own painful memories, and—because he is not just Christ crucified but Christ resurrected—companions us, attends us, heals us by infusing us with his very self, exchanging the darkness of our lives with his own glorious light.

God's grace, moreover, gravitates *toward*—rather than being repelled by—sin. Recall the story about Simon,[28] acting all self-righteous and indignant when Jesus allowed a sinful woman to carry on in a sloppy, emotional, even sensual display of gratitude. And Jesus helped him to see that the person who has been forgiven most loves most. Similarly, those who suffer greatly, and whose suffering has been greatly redeemed by the grace of God, are most grateful.

As we tally-mark our days, adding up the years which grow into decades, we often experience the aging process as a series of losses, followed by a string of griefs, when the gift it actually affords is more time, more opportunities to receive grace, increasing our capacity to love and to be loved. If there is but one prayer remaining on our lips when the light goes out of our eyes, when the world becomes hush, when time is stilled at the end of our days, *thank you* will suffice. With the availability of grace in such abundance now, it wouldn't hurt us to practice it now.

Grace and peace,
Pastor Eric

ANCHORITE

Trust in the Lord *forever,*
for in the Lord God
you have an everlasting rock.
ISAIAH 26:4

Recently, while roaming the hills above Saint Gertrude's, a modest Benedictine monastery overlooking the Camas Prairie, I heard myself saying out loud, for only the trees and the birds to hear, "I've never been here before." It's true; I had never been to this particular place in Cottonwood, Idaho. But it was also true that the "I" that is Eric had never been in this frame of mind, this state of soul. I wasn't lost and I wasn't disoriented (nor am I now), but it was new territory nonetheless. I have never lived in a world my dad didn't occupy. But now I do. I've never been here before.

Whoever said "some things never change" was either lying or just dead wrong. Everything and everyone changes. Nothing and no one remains the same. The task of life, it seems to me, is to learn to navigate and to integrate these changes, for they are the raw material for becoming our true, full selves. As the changes pile up, and as we adapt to them and internalize them, our souls expand. Our capacity as containers of Life enlarges.

But when the change is big, unsettling, unwelcome, when it causes the ground underfoot to shift, when it's difficult to discern true north, it is helpful to have points of stability. I call them *anchor points*; it is, for me, not a nautical term but a mountaineering image. The thing about anchors, whether they are fastened into rock or ice, is that once they are secure ("bomber" in the climbing vernacular), and once you learn to trust them, they give you great freedom to take risks. You can venture out into unknown, even dangerous areas, knowing that the anchor will catch and hold you if you fall.

I have a three-point anchor system that holds my life.

Baptism: I have been reclaimed by lethal and life-giving waters. My old self is dead. I am a new creation. Joined to the Living Waters, I have been given a new name, a new identity, and a new purpose. In baptism, I join the priesthood of all believers. I am blessed, and I am a blessing.

Ordination: The church has set me apart as a priest among the priesthood to be a minister of *Word* and *Sacrament.* These are the primary tools of my vocation, chock full of grace and truth. They are the effective, sacred means I have been entrusted with in order to lead a congregation in the way of Jesus.

Marriage: I am living my years joined intimately to one person who both knows me the best and loves me the most. We honor our vows to love and to cherish each other no matter what. We practice daily the mutuality of grace and forgiveness.

This is my sacred trinity of trustworthy anchors.

It's significant to me that my dad established me in all three of them:

He got me wet in the sacramental waters at my baptism on an Easter Sunday morning.

He laid hands on me and offered the prayer at my ordination on a Maryland evening.

He oversaw the occasion when Elizabeth and I exchanged our solemn marriage vows on the shore of Flathead Lake one summer afternoon.

In each case, he set the anchors and then gave me the freedom to learn them, to grow into them, and to move out from them. But he didn't leave me alone to merely figure it out all by myself. He modeled for me the life of discipleship, the pastoral vocation, the mysteries of marriage.

When everything else shifts, changes, or erupts, I am held in this internal monastery of stability and security, anchoring me to that which matters eternally. Here I can rest in peace. And from here I can courageously venture.

Thanks be to God for Eugene H. Peterson, the man who not only got me started but the one who showed me the Way.

Grace and peace,
Pastor Eric

LEAVE A TRACE

We are God's workmanship, created in Christ Jesus for good works.
EPHESIANS 2:10, EHV

WITH MY NEW TITANIUM hip securely fastened to and fully integrated into my skeletal system, I am eagerly looking forward to trail-testing it this month on Mount Rainier's well-named Wonderland Trail with my three big kids and my brother, Leif. If the trip goes according to plan, we will use the Fryingpan Creek trailhead to access the wondrous trail, and, over three or four days, hike our way around the south side of the mountain, traversing Ohanapecosh Park and ending up at Paradise (the best place to eat a cheeseburger!). And you can bet that, except for the photographs and eyewitnesses along the way, no one will ever know that we had been there.

With the ecological movement of the 1970s coinciding with my tenure as a Boy Scout came a phrase that has been drilled into my conscious mind as indelibly as the Scriptures

I have memorized over the years. It started out as "Take Nothing but Pictures, Leave Nothing but Footprints." But in more recent years, it has been abbreviated and canonized by both the Sierra Club and some federal agencies into the succinct motto: "Leave No Trace." Whether visiting the backcountry or the frontcountry, there should be no physical evidence that you were ever there. Head for the hills, enjoy a trail, or camp in an alpine meadow, but do it in a way that nobody following you would notice that you'd been there. We must all do what we can to preserve what precious little is left of our pristine environment.

While this is good advice as we relate to the planet, it does not transfer well to our relationship with the Kingdom of God. When we pray, "Thy kingdom come," we are essentially assenting to being agents for that purpose—helping to bring about that reality of which Christ is king. The clash of values between the kingdom of this world and God's Kingdom is stark and fierce, and it needs people who can show us how to live according to its code of conduct as citizens of the Way. Unfortunately, far too many people are remembered for things that have little or no eternal significance.

I'm not planning on dying anytime soon, but I am trying to live as someone who is prepared to die. And when that time comes, I would like to think that I will have had something to show for myself, a life well-lived, a gift more generously offered than selfishly squandered, one that, through words and deeds, in fits and starts, pointed to the reality of the inbreaking Kingdom of God and the indwelling Son of God. Moreover, I sincerely hope that I am eulogized as someone who helped a community of people become more God-attentive.

When it comes to trails, tread lightly and leave a faint footprint. But when it comes to influence, live your life in such a way that it leaves the high-impact marks and telltale signs of the Kingdom of God. Leave a trace of truth. Leave an indelible legacy of love.

Grace and peace,
Pastor Eric

EPILOGUE
Identity and Purpose

We are His workmanship, created in Christ Jesus for good works.
EPHESIANS 2:10, NASB

I'VE BEEN NOTICING, and have become convicted lately, that around certain people, my story can sound somewhat clumsy. For example, when I'm meeting someone for the first time, they might ask, "So, how many kids do you have?" Beginning with my own hesitation about whether the answer is "three" or "six," and sometimes accompanied by "well, it depends on how you do the math," or "it's a little complicated," my own awkwardness reveals that I have not fully integrated my own messy, marvelous story of redemption.[1]

Similarly, I've noticed that when people ask me what I do for a living, my response can vary a bit depending on who I'm talking to. It's simple when speaking to a person of faith, and I answer in a straightforward way: "I'm a pastor." When I gave that response to the woman sitting next to me on a plane last month, it was met with instant recognition and enthusiasm, and she immediately started telling me all about herself, assuming that I was interested in her story and that I was a safe person to tell it to, both of which, I'd like to think, were true.

But that's not always the response I get. I recall riding up a ski lift one winter afternoon with a twenty-something young man. I found out that he was an engineer for Boeing, and as he explained to me what was involved in his job, I had a pretty good sense of what he did in overseeing wing construction. But after he asked me what I did for a living, and I said, "I'm a pastor," he turned to me, lifted up his ski mask so as to give me a clear view of his scrunched-up expression, and asked, "What in the world is that?" He had never heard the word before, and he had no idea what was involved.

To try to explain to him that I am driven by issues of theology, Christology, pneumatology, ecclesiology, and soteriology would have been meaningless. After all, he had never heard such words before, and he was getting along just fine with his life, thank you very much. How does one compare the value of such things as preaching, praying, pastoral care, and the sacraments to someone who doesn't even have room for God in his worldview? How do you describe the importance of the Bible (a collection of books that apparently contradicts itself, eludes understanding, and is the unending source of debate and controversy) to someone who is accustomed to working with the precision of an installation manual? Why would I identify myself as a leader of a congregation when the church has historically made so many mistakes and done so much damage?

What do you do? "I'm on a team that's designing and

building the next generation of aircraft that will transport people on nonstop transcontinental flights."

What do *you* do? "Uh, well I proclaim Good News and care for people in the name of Jesus, and I get babies wet." Can you see why I sometimes question the practical value and importance of my vocation, especially with those who don't share a common faith?

When I asked a non-Christian friend of mine—a retired electrician—to help me with a wiring project at my house recently, I suggested that we barter a trade. This was his response: "I don't think I need any of the services you provide. I'm already happily married, and I'm not planning to die anytime soon."

Really? Is that all I'm good for? What in the world, indeed.

To compensate, I have basic skills in carpentry and plumbing. I know how to cut down a tree and plow snow. I can repair small engines and install irrigation systems.

Still, even though it may not look like much to some people, I have never been clearer that to live my vocational life as a pastor is what I was made for, participating with God in acts of reconciliation, healing, justice. Living the way of grace and truth. Following the rhythms of life and death. Doing the hard work of love.

I'm not ready to completely put away my tools or retire my truck, but I think I shall just stick with what I was called and ordained to do twenty-two years ago. I'll keep witnessing, in word and in deed, to the Good News. I will continue to celebrate the sacramental reality of God-with-us, as I lift up bread and cup and splash water on the heads of saints young and old. And I will offer my meager gifts in service to the holy agenda of redemption, in anticipation of the day when Jesus will return, setting to rights all that is wrong, creating a new heaven and a new earth. What in the world could be more practical than that?

Grace and peace,
Pastor Eric

NOTES

INTRODUCTION

1. Galatians 3:1, MSG.
2. Philippians 1:3, MSG.

1: WHAT MY LIFE IS ABOUT

1. Psalm 24:1, KJV.
2. Thomas Moore, *Meditations: On the Monk Who Dwells in Daily Life* (New York: HarperCollins, 1994), 65.
3. John 8:32, MEV.
4. Psalm 40:3.
5. The Beach Boys, "Kokomo," *Kokomo* © Elektra 1988.
6. Edwin Hatch, "Breathe on Me, Breath of God," 1878.
7. Genesis 32:28, meaning of Israel (see AMPC).
8. Genesis 35:29, referring to Isaac.
9. Sam wrote this poem as a gift to me. He is now deceased, and I include the poem here in his memory.
10. C. S. Lewis, *The Problem of Pain* (New York; HarperCollins, 2001), 91.
11. From the Apostles' Creed.
12. Walter Brueggemann, *Spirituality of the Psalms* (Minneapolis, MN: Fortress Press, 2002).
13. Sara Groves, "Love Is Still a Worthy Cause," *Tell Me What You Know* (INO Records, 2007).
14. Joan D. Chittister, *Scarred by Struggle, Transformed by Hope* (Grand Rapids, MI: Eerdmans, 2003), 59.

2: WHAT GOD IS ABOUT

1. James Hollis, *Finding Meaning in the Second Half of Life: How to Finally,* Really *Grow Up* (New York: Gotham, 2005), chap. 8.

2. As quoted in Ronald Rolheiser, "Our Unfinished Symphony," August 19, 2007, https://ronrolheiser.com/our-unfinished-symphony/#.XQftoi3Myu4.
3. For an article that discusses the species of fish that actually inhabit the Sea of Galilee, see https://ferrelljenkins.blog/2014/12/01/fish-of-the-sea-of-galilee/.
4. This reference is to a generalized cultural anxiety in late 2012 that because December marked the end of an ancient Mayan calendar, it might thus usher in the end of the world.
5. Y2K is shorthand for a generalized cultural anxiety that a technological glitch in how dates are recorded in software would cause widespread societal collapse as the calendar shifted from 1999 to 2000.
6. Harold Camping died in December 2013 at age ninety-two, after repeatedly predicting the end of the world.
7. Luke 2:12.
8. John 3:1-21.
9. Philippians 2:5-8.
10. Luke 2:19.
11. Charles Wesley, "Come, Thou Long-Expected Jesus," 1744. Emphasis added.
12. Robert Wuthnow, *After Heaven: Spirituality in America Since the 1950s* (Berkeley: University of California Press, 1998), 121.
13. Hebrews 13:2.
14. Michael D. C. Drout, ed., *J. R. R. Tolkien Encyclopedia: Scholarship and Critical Assessment* (New York: Routledge, 2007), 176.
15. Randy Butler and Terry Butler, "At the Cross" (Mercy/Vineyard Publishing, 1993).
16. Romans 8:1.
17. 1 Corinthians 4:10.
18. Matthew 16:25.

3: WHAT THE CHURCH IS ABOUT

1. Herbert Thurston, "Bells," *The Catholic Encyclopedia*, vol. 2 (New York: Robert Appleton Company, 1907), accessed July 5, 2019, http://www.newadvent.org/cathen/02418b.htm.
2. See Romans 10:17.
3. Exodus 20:8.
4. Thurston, "Bells," *The Catholic Encyclopedia*, 421.
5. Matthew 5:13, MSG.
6. See Hebrews 13:8.

7. See John 14:6.
8. Eleanor Hull, versifier, "Be Thou My Vision," 1912.
9. See Ephesians 4:4-6.
10. See Revelation 5:9; 14:3.
11. Statistics were current as of 2012, when this newsletter was written. See "Prison Population," OECD Library, accessed October 23, 2019, https://read.oecd-ilibrary.org/social-issues-migration-health/oecd-factbook-2010/prison-population_factbook-2010-95-en#page4; "Water Consumption," OECD Library, accessed October 23, 2019, https://read.oecd-ilibrary.org/economics/oecd-factbook-2011-2012/water-consumption_factbook-2011-76-en#page1; "Air and GHG Emissions," OECD.org, accessed October 23, 2019, https://data.oecd.org/air/air-and-ghg-emissions.htm; and "Intentional Homicides," OECD Library, accessed October 23, 2019, https://read.oecd-ilibrary.org/economics/how-s-life/intentional-homicides_9789264121164-graph112-en#page1.
12. "Presbyterians and the American Revolution," Presbyterian Historical Society, accessed October 22, 2019, https://www.history.pcusa.org/history-online/exhibits/presbyterians-and-american-revolution-page-1.
13. In chronological order: Andrew Jackson, James Polk, James Buchanan, Grover Cleveland, Benjamin Harrison, Woodrow Wilson, Dwight Eisenhower, and Ronald Reagan. See https://www.pewforum.org/2009/01/15/the-religious-affiliations-of-us-presidents/.
14. As quoted in William J. Duiker and Jackson J. Spielvogel, *The Essential World History*, third ed. (Belmont, CA: Thomas Wadsworth, 2008), 314.
15. Genesis 22:17.
16. Acts 15:39. The split between Paul and Barnabas had to do with whether Mark was fit to be included in their ministry.
17. 2 Timothy 4:11. Paul's praise of Mark's ministry is broadly understood to represent reconciliation between him and Paul (and Barnabas).
18. "'Truthiness': Can Something 'Seem,' without Being, True?" Merriam-Webster, April 18, 2019, https://www.merriam-webster.com/words-at-play/truthiness-meaning-word-origin.
19. See John 1:14.
20. John 1:3.
21. Ephesians 6:4, KJV.
22. Mark 9:42; see also Luke 17:2.
23. Luke 18:16.
24. Audrey Schulman, "How to Be a Climate Hero," *Orion Magazine*, April 23, 2008, https://orionmagazine.org/article/how-to-be-a-climate-hero/.

25. "The Bystander Effect," Economic and Social Research Council, accessed October 22, 2019, https://esrc.ukri.org/about-us/50-years-of-esrc/50-achievements/the-bystander-effect/.
26. Matthew 12:50; Mark 3:35.
27. Matthew 7:7-8.
28. Genesis 1:3; John 11:43.
29. John 1:14, MSG.
30. Hebrews 13:8.

4: WHAT FOLLOWING JESUS IS ABOUT

1. Matthew 7:20.
2. John Muir, *Our National Parks* (Boston: Houghton Mifflin, 1916), 3.
3. From the American folk song "Pick a Bale of Cotton." This song has racist undertones. I grew up south of the Mason-Dixon Line in the 1960s.
4. Mark 16:15.
5. I've here rendered in the first-person an anecdote about Louis IX. Read the anecdote in M. Cecilia Gaposchkin and Sean L. Field, *The Sanctity of Louis IX: Early Lives of Saint Louis by Geoffrey of Beaulieu and William of Chartres,* trans. Larry F. Field (Ithaca, NY: Cornell University Press, 2014), 111–12.
6. Exodus 19:6.
7. John 20:21.
8. Ernest Hemingway, *A Farewell to Arms* (New York: Scribner, 2014), 318.
9. Thanks to singer Sara Groves for the phrase "add to the beauty," from her album *Add to the Beauty* (Sony, 2005).
10. Romans 8:28.
11. Psalm 90:4.
12. Cyprian, *The Good of Patience* in *The Fathers of the Church: St. Cyprian Treatises* (Washington DC: Catholic University of America Press, 2007), 280.
13. Galatians 5:22.
14. 1 Corinthians 12:31; 13:1, emphasis added.
15. Ephesians 4:13.
16. See, for example, Matthew 23:27-28; James 1:21-26; and 1 John 4:20 (hypocrisy); Proverbs 14:31; 1 Thessalonians 4:6; and 2 Peter 2:3 (exploitation); and Luke 13:3 (stubbornness).
17. Luke 17:2.
18. Matthew 18:3.
19. John 3:5.
20. 1 John 3:2, MSG.

21. Barbara Johnson, *Boomerang Joy: Joy that Goes Around, Comes Around* (Grand Rapids, MI: Zondervan, 1998), 167.
22. Isaiah 6:8.
23. Luke 1:18.
24. Jerome, Letter CXXX, to Demetrias, in Philip Schaff and Henry Wace, eds., *A Select Library of the Nicene and Post-Nicene Fathers of the Christian Church*, vol. 6, *St. Jerome: Letters and Select Works* (New York: The Christian Literature Company, 1893), 266.
25. Quintus Tertullianus, *On Repentance* (Savage, MN: Lighthouse, 2015), 11–12.
26. Matthew 13:52.
27. Saint Augustine, *Confessions*, trans. Henry Chadwick (Oxford: Oxford University Press, 2008), 3.
28. Luke 7:36-50.

EPILOGUE

1. My wife Elizabeth and I each brought three children to our marriage.

YOU'LL ALSO ENJOY

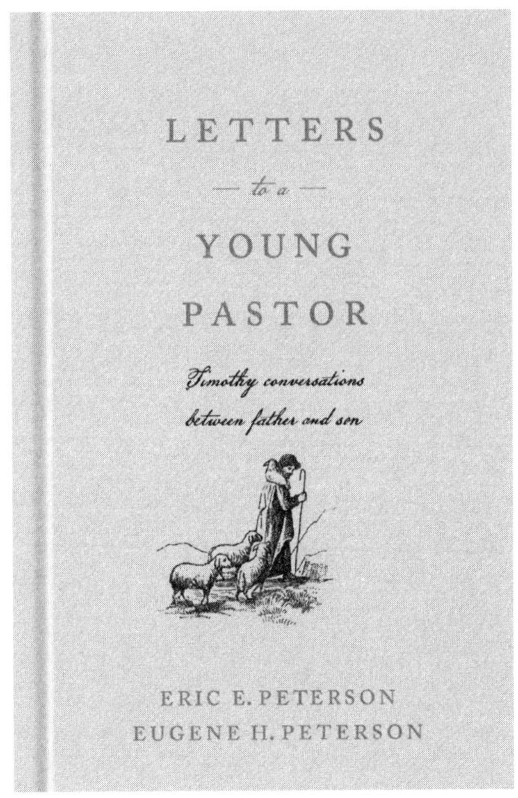

Letters to a Young Pastor is a compilation of letters written to Eric by Eugene Peterson. You'll find the book ripe with advice, encouragement, and mentoring with respect to the pastoral life.

THE NAVIGATORS® STORY

THANK YOU for picking up this NavPress book! I hope it has been a blessing to you.

NavPress is a ministry of The Navigators. The Navigators began in the 1930s, when a young California lumberyard worker named Dawson Trotman was impacted by basic discipleship principles and felt called to teach those principles to others. He saw this mission as an echo of 2 Timothy 2:2: "And the things you have heard me say in the presence of many witnesses entrust to reliable people who will also be qualified to teach others" (NIV).

In 1933, Trotman and his friends began discipling members of the US Navy. By the end of World War II, thousands of men on ships and bases around the world were learning the principles of spiritual multiplication by the intentional, person-to-person teaching of God's Word.

After World War II, The Navigators expanded its relational ministry to include college campuses; local churches; the Glen Eyrie Conference Center and Eagle Lake Camps in Colorado Springs, Colorado; and neighborhood and citywide initiatives across the country and around the world.

Today, with more than 2,600 US staff members—and local ministries in more than 100 countries—The Navigators continues the transformational process of making disciples who make more disciples, advancing the Kingdom of God in a world that desperately needs the hope and salvation of Jesus Christ and the encouragement to grow deeper in relationship with Him.

NavPress was created in 1975 to advance the calling of The Navigators by bringing biblically rooted and culturally relevant products to people who want to know and love Christ more deeply. In January 2014, NavPress entered an alliance with Tyndale House Publishers to strengthen and better position our rich content for the future. Through *THE MESSAGE* Bible and other resources, NavPress seeks to bring positive spiritual movement to people's lives.

If you're interested in learning more or becoming involved with The Navigators, go to www.navigators.org. For more discipleship content from The Navigators and NavPress authors, visit www.thedisciplemaker.org. May God bless you in your walk with Him!

Sincerely,

DON PAPE
VP/PUBLISHER, NAVPRESS

www.navpress.com

CP1308